Odes & Elegies by Michael Drayton

Michael Drayton was born in 1563 at Hartshill, near Nuneaton, Warwickshire, England. The facts of his early life remain unknown.

Drayton first published, in 1590, a volume of spiritual poems; The Harmony of the Church. Ironically the Archbishop of Canterbury seized almost the entire edition and had it destroyed.

In 1593 he published Idea: The Shepherd's Garland, 9 pastorals celebrating his own love-sorrows under the poetic name of Rowland. This was later expanded to a 64 sonnet cycle.

With the publication of The Legend of Piers Gaveston, Matilda and Mortimeriados, later enlarged and re-published, in 1603, under the title of The Barons' Wars. His career began to gather interest and attention.

In 1596, The Legend of Robert, Duke of Normandy, another historical poem was published, followed in 1597 by England's Heroical Epistles, a series of historical studies, in imitation of those of Ovid. Written in the heroic couplet, they contain some of his finest writing.

Like other poets of his era, Drayton wrote for the theatre; but unlike Shakespeare, Jonson, or Samuel Daniel, he invested little of his art in the genre. Between 1597 and 1602, Drayton was a member of the stable of playwrights who worked for Philip Henslowe. Henslowe's Diary links Drayton's name with 23 plays from that period, and, for all but one unfinished work, in collaboration with others such as Thomas Dekker, Anthony Munday, and Henry Chettle. Only one play has survived; Part 1 of Sir John Oldcastle, which Drayton wrote with Munday, Robert Wilson, and Richard Hathwaye but little of Drayton can be seen in its pages.

By this time, as a poet, Drayton was well received and admired at the Court of Elizabeth 1st. If he hoped to continue that admiration with the accession of James 1st he thought wrong. In 1603, he addressed a poem of compliment to James I, but it was ridiculed, and his services rudely rejected.

In 1605 Drayton reprinted his most important works; the historical poems and the Idea. Also published was a fantastic satire called The Man in the Moon and, for the for the first time the famous Ballad of Agincourt.

Since 1598 he had worked on Poly-Olbion, a work to celebrate all the points of topographical or antiquarian interest in Great Britain. Eighteen books in total, the first were published in 1614 and the last in 1622.

In 1627 he published another of his miscellaneous volumes. In it Drayton printed The Battle of Agincourt (an historical poem but not to be confused with his ballad on the same subject), The Miseries of Queen Margaret, and the acclaimed Nimphidia, the Court of Faery, as well as several other important pieces.

Drayton last published in 1630 with The Muses' Elizium.

Michael Drayton died in London on December 23rd, 1631. He was buried in Westminster Abbey, in Poets' Corner. A monument was placed there with memorial lines attributed to Ben Jonson.

Index of Contents

ODES

TO HIMSELFE AND THE HARPE

And why not I, as hee
That's greatest, if as free,
(In sundry strains that striue,
Since there so many be)
Th' old Lyrick kind reuiue?

I will, yea, and I may;
Who shall oppose my way?
For what is he alone,
That of himselfe can say,
Hee's Heire of Helicon?

APOLLO, and the Nine,
Forbid no Man their Shrine,
That commeth with hands pure;
Else be they so diuine,
They will not him indure.

For they be such coy Things,
That they care not for Kings,
And dare let them know it;
Nor may he touch their Springs,
That is not borne a Poet.

The Phocean it did proue,
Whom when foule Lust did move,
Those Mayds unchast to make,
Fell, as with them he strove,
His Neck and justly brake.

That instrument ne'r heard,
Strooke by the skilfull Bard,
It strongly to awake;
But it th' infernalls skard,
And made Olympus quake.

As those Prophetike strings
Whose sounds with fiery Wings,
Drave Fiends from their abode,
Touch'd by the best of Kings,
That sang the holy Ode.

So his, which Women slue,
And it int' Hebrus threw,
Such sounds yet forth it sent,
The Bankes to weepe that drue,
As downe the streame it went.

That by the Tortoyse shell,
To MAYAS Sonne it fell,
The most thereof not doubt
But sure some Power did dwell,
In Him who found it out.

The Wildest of the field,
And Ayre, with Riuers t' yeeld,
Which mou'd; that sturdy Glebes,
And massie Oakes could weeld,
To rayse the pyles of Thebes.

And diversly though Strung,
So anciently We sung,
To it, that Now scarce knowne,
If first it did belong
To Greece, or if our Owne.

The Druydes imbrew'd,
With Gore, on Altars rude
With Sacrifices crown'd,
In hollow Woods bedew'd,
Ador'd the Trembling sound.

Though wee be All to seeke,
Of PINDAR that Great Greeke,
To Finger it aright,
The Soule with power to strike,
His hand retayn'd such Might.

Or him that Rome did grace
Whose Ayres we all imbrace,
That scarcely found his Peere,
Nor giueth PHŒBVS place,
For Strokes diuinely cleere.

The Irish I admire,
And still cleave to that Lyre,
As our Musike's Mother,
And thinke, till I expire,
APOLLO'S such another.

As Britons, that so long
Have held this Antike Song,
And let all our Carpers
Forbeare their fame to wrong,
Th' are right skilfull Harpers.

Southerne, I long thee spare,
Yet wish thee well to fare,
Who me pleased'st greatly,
As first, therefore more rare,
Handling thy Harpe neatly.

To those that with despight
Shall terme these Numbers slight,
Tell them their Iudgement's blind,
Much erring from the right,
It is a Noble kind.

Nor is 't the Verse doth make,
That giveth, or doth take,
'Tis possible to clyme,
To kindle, or to slake,
Although in SKELTON'S Ryme.

TO THE NEW YEERE

Rich Statue, double-faced,
With Marble Temples graced,
To rayse thy God-head hyer,
In flames where Altars shining,
Before thy Priests diuining,
Doe od'rous Fumes expire.

Great IANVS, I thy pleasure,
With all the Thespian treasure,
Doe seriously pursue;
To th' passed yeere returning,
As though the old adiourning,
Yet bringing in the new.

Thy ancient Vigils yeerely,
I have observed cleerely,
Thy Feasts yet smoaking bee;
Since all thy store abroad is,
Give something to my Goddesse,
As hath been us'd by thee.

Give her th' Eoan brightnesse,
Wing'd with that subtill lightnesse,
That doth trans-pierce the Ayre;
The Roses of the Morning
The rising Heav'n adorning,

To mesh with flames of Hayre.

Those ceaselesse Sounds, above all,
Made by those Orbes that move all,
And ever swelling there,
Wrap'd up in Numbers flowing,
Them actually bestowing,
For Iewels at her Eare.

O Rapture great and holy,
Doe thou transport me wholly,
So well her forme to vary,
That I aloft may beare her,
Whereas I will insphere her,
In Regions high and starry.

And in my choise Composures,
The soft and easie Closures,
So amorously shall meet;
That every liuely Ceasure
Shall tread a perfect Measure
Set on so equall feet.

That Spray to fame so fertle,
The Lover-crowning Mirtle,
In Wreaths of mixed Bowes,
Within whose shades are dwelling
Those Beauties most excelling,
Inthron'd upon her Browes.

Those Paralels so even,
Drawne on the face of Heaven,
That curious Art supposes,
Direct those Gems, whose cleerenesse
Farre off amaze by neerenesse,
Each Globe such fire incloses.

Her Bosome full of Blisses,
By Nature made for Kisses,
So pure and wond'rous cleere,
Whereas a thousand Graces
Behold their lovely Faces,
As they are bathing there.

O, thou selfe-little blindnesse,
The kindnesse of unkindnesse,
Yet one of those diuine;
Thy Brands to me were lever,

Thy Fascia, and thy Quiuer,
And thou this Quill of mine.

This Heart so freshly bleeding,
Upon it owne selfe feeding,
Whose woundes still dropping be;
O Loue, thy selfe confounding,
Her coldnesse so abounding,
And yet such heat in me.

Yet if I be inspired,
Ile leave thee so admired,
To all that shall succeed,
That were they more then many,
'Mongst all, there is not any,
That Time so oft shall read.

Nor Adamant ingraved,
That hath been choisely 'st saved,
IDEA'S Name out-weares;
So large a Dower as this is,
The greatest often misses,
The Diadem that beares.

TO HIS VALENTINE

Muse, bid the Morne awake,
Sad Winter now declines,
Each Bird doth chuse a Make,
This day 's Saint VALENTINE'S;
For that good Bishop's sake
Get up, and let us see,
What Beautie it shall bee,
That Fortune us assignes.

But lo, in happy How'r,
The place wherein she lyes,
In yonder climbing Tow'r,
Gilt by the glitt'ring Rise;
O JOVE! that in a Show'r,
As once that Thund'rer did,
When he in drops lay hid,
That I could her surprize.

Her Canopie Ile draw,
With spangled Plumes bedight,

No Mortall ever saw
So rauishing a sight;
That it the Gods might awe,
And pow'rfully trans-pierce
The Globie Vniuerse,
Out-shooting eu'ry Light.

My Lips Ile softly lay
Vpon her heau'nly Cheeke,
Dy'd like the dawning Day,
As polish'd Iuorie sleeke:
And in her Eare Ile say;
O, thou bright Morning-Starre,
'Tis I that come so farre,
My Valentine to seeke.

Each little Bird, this Tyde,
Doth chuse her loved Pheere,
Which constantly abide
In Wedlock all the yeere,
As Nature is their Guide:
So may we two be true,
This yeere, nor change for new,
As Turtles coupled were.

The Sparrow, Swan, the Doue,
Though VENUS Birds they be,
Yet are they not for Loue
So absolute as we:
For Reason us doth moue;
They but by billing woo:
Then try what we can doo,
To whom each sense is free.

Which we have more then they,
By livelyer Organs sway'd,
Our Appetite each way
More by our Sense obay'd:
Our Passions to display,
This Season us doth fit;
Then let us follow it,
As Nature us doth lead.

One Kisse in two let's breake,
Confounded with the touch,
But halfe words let us speake,
Our Lip's imploy'd so much,
Vntill we both grow weake,

With sweetnesse of thy breath;
O smother me to death:
Long let our Ioyes be such.

Let's laugh at them that chuse
Their Valentines by lot,
To weare their Names that use,
Whom idly they have got:
Such poore choise we refuse,
Saint VALENTINE befriend;
We thus this Morne may spend,
Else Muse, awake her not.

THE HEART

If thus we needs must goe,
What shall our one Heart doe,
This One made of our Two?

Madame, two Hearts we brake,
And from them both did take
The best, one Heart to make.

Halfe this is of your Heart,
Mine in the other part,
Ioyn'd by our equall Art.

Were it cymented, or sowne,
By Shreds or Pieces knowne,
We each might find our owne.

But 'tis dissolv'd, and fix'd,
And with such cunning mix'd,
No diffrence that betwixt.

But how shall we agree,
By whom it kept shall be,
Whether by you, or me?

It cannot two Brests fill,
One must be heartlesse still,
Vntill the other will.

It came to me one day,
When I will'd it to say,
With whether it would stay?

It told me, in your Brest,
Where it might hope to rest:
For if it were my Ghest,

For certainety it knew,
That I would still anew
Be sending it to you.

Never, I thinke, had two
Such worke, so much to doo,
A Vnitie to woo.

Yours was so cold and chaste,
Whilst mine with zeale did waste,
Like Fire with Water plac'd.

How did my Heart intreat,
How pant, how did it beat,
Till it could giue yours heat!

Till to that temper brought,
Through our perfection wrought,
That blessing eythers Thought.

In such a Height it lyes,
From this base Worlds dull Eyes,
That Heaven it not enuyes.

All that this Earth can show,
Our Heart shall not once know,
For it too vile and low.

THE SACRIFICE TO APOLLO

Priests of APOLLO, sacred be the Roome,
For this learn'd Meeting: Let no barbarous Groome,
How brave soe'r he bee,
Attempt to enter;
But of the Muses free,
None here may venter;
This for the Delphian Prophets is prepar'd:
The prophane Vulgar are from hence debar'd.

And since the Feast so happily begins,
Call up those faire Nine, with their Violins;

They are begot by JOVE,
Then let us place them,
Where no Clowne in may shoue,
That may disgrace them:
But let them neere to young APOLLO sit;
So shall his Foot-pace ouer-flow with Wit.

Where be the Graces, where be those fayre Three?
In any hand they may not absent bee:
They to the Gods are deare,
And they can humbly
Teach us, our Selues to beare,
And doe things comely:
They, and the Muses, rise both from one Stem,
They grace the Muses, and the Muses them.

Bring forth your Flaggons (fill'd with sparkling Wine)
Whereon swolne BACCHUS, crowned with a Vine,
Is graven, and fill out,
It well bestowing,
To ev'ry Man about,
In Goblets flowing:
Let not a Man drinke, but in Draughts profound;
To our God PHŒBUS let the Health goe Round.

Let your Iests flye at large; yet therewithall
See they be Salt, but yet not mix'd with Gall:
Not tending to disgrace,
But fayrely given,
Becomming well the place,
Modest, and euen;
That they with tickling Pleasure may prouoke
Laughter in him, on whom the Iest is broke.

Or if the deeds of HEROES ye rehearse,
Let them be sung in so well-ord'red Verse,
That each word have his weight,
Yet runne with pleasure;
Holding one stately height,
In so brave measure,
That they may make the stiffest Storme seeme weake,
And dampe JOVES Thunder, when it lowd'st doth speake.

And if yee list to exercise your Vayne,
Or in the Sock, or in the Buskin'd Strayne,
Let Art and Nature goe
One with the other;
Yet so, that Art may show

Nature her Mother;
The thick-brayn'd Audience liuely to awake,
Till with shrill Claps the Theater doe shake.

Sing Hymnes to BACCHUS then, with hands uprear'd,
Offer to JOVE, who most is to be fear'd;
From him the Muse we have,
From him proceedeth
More then we dare to crave;
'Tis he that feedeth
Them, whom the World would starue; then let the Lyre
Sound, whilst his Altars endlesse flames expire.

TO CUPID

Maydens, why spare ye?
Or whether not dare ye
Correct the blind Shooter?
Because wanton VENUS,
So oft that doth paine us,
Is her Sonnes Tutor.

Now in the Spring,
He proveth his Wing,
The Field is his Bower,
And as the small Bee,
About flyeth hee,
From Flower to Flower.

And wantonly roves,
Abroad in the Groves,
And in the Ayre hovers,
Which when it him deweth,
His Fethers he meweth,
In sighes of true Lovers.

And since doom'd by Fate,
(That well knew his Hate)
That Hee should be blinde;
For very despite,
Our Eyes be his White,
So wayward his kinde.

If his Shafts loosing,
(Ill his Mark choosing)
Or his Bow broken;

The Moane VENUS maketh,
And care that she taketh,
Cannot be spoken.

To VULCAN commending
Her love, and straight sending
Her Doues and her Sparrowes,
With Kisses unto him,
And all but to woo him,
To make her Sonne Arrowes.

Telling what he hath done,
(Sayth she, Right mine owne Sonne)
In her Armes she him closes,
Sweetes on him fans,
Layd in Downe of her Swans,
His Sheets, Leaves of Roses.

And feeds him with Kisses;
Which oft when he misses,
He ever is froward:
The Mothers o'r-joying,
Makes by much coying,
The Child so untoward.

Yet in a fine Net,
That a Spider set,
The Maydens had caught him;
Had she not beene neere him,
And chanced to heare him,
More good they had taught him.

AN AMOURET ANACREONTICK

Most good, most faire,
Or Thing as rare,
To call you's lost;
For all the cost
Words can bestow,
So poorely show
Upon your prayse,
That all the wayes
Sense hath, come short:
Whereby Report
Falls them under;
That when Wonder

More hath seyzed,
Yet not pleased,
That it in kinde
Nothing can finde,
You to expresse:
Neverthelesse,
As by Globes small,
This Mightie ALL
Is shew'd, though farre
From Life, each Starre
A World being:
So wee seeing
You, like as that,
Onely trust what
Art doth us teach;
And when I reach
At Morall Things,
And that my Strings
Gravely should strike,
Straight some mislike
Blotteth mine ODE.
As with the Loade,
The Steele we touch,
Forced ne'r so much,
Yet still remoues
To that it loves,
Till there it stayes;
So to your prayse
I turne ever,
And though never
From you mouing,
Happie so loving.

LOVES CONQUEST

Wer't granted me to choose,
How I would end my dayes;
Since I this life must loose,
It should be in Your praise;
For there is no Bayes
Can be set above you.

S' impossibly I love You,
And for you sit so hie,
Whence none may remove You
In my cleere Poesie,

That I oft deny
You so ample Merit.

The freedome of my Spirit
Maintayning (still) my Cause,
Your Sex not to inherit,
Urging the Salique Lawes;
But your Vertue drawes
From me every due.

Thus still You me pursue,
That no where I can dwell,
By Feare made just to You,
Who naturally rebell,
Of You that excell
That should I still Endyte,

Yet will You want some Ryte.
That lost in your high praise
I wander to and fro,
As seeing sundry Waies:
Yet which the right not know
To get out of this Maze.

TO THE VIRIGINIAN VOYAGE

You brave Heroique minds,
Worthy your Countries Name;
That Honour still pursue,
Goe, and subdue,
Whilst loyt'ring Hinds
Lurke here at home, with shame.

Britans, you stay too long,
Quickly aboard bestow you,
And with a merry Gale
Swell your stretch'd Sayle,
With Vowes as strong,
As the Winds that blow you.

Your Course securely steere,
West and by South forth keepe,
Rocks, Lee-shores, nor Sholes,
When EOLUS scowles,
You need not feare,
So absolute the Deepe.

And cheerefully at Sea,
Successe you still intice,
To get the Pearle and Gold,
And ours to hold,
VIRGINIA,
Earth's onely Paradise.

Where Nature hath in store
Fowle, Venison, and Fish,
And the Fruitfull'st Soyle,
Without your Toyle,
Three Haruests more,
All greater then your Wish.

And the ambitious Vine
Crownes with his purple Masse,
The cedar reaching hie
To kisse the Sky
The Cypresse, Pine
And use-full Sassafras.

To whome, the golden Age
Still Natures lawes doth give,
No other Cares that tend,
But Them to defend
From Winters rage,
That long there doth not live.

When as the Lushious smell
Of that delicious Land,
Above the Seas that flowes,
The cleere Wind throwes,
Your Hearts to swell
Approaching the deare Strande.

In kenning of the Shore
(Thanks to God first given,)
O you the happy'st men,
Be Frolike then,
Let Cannons roare,
Frighting the wide Heaven.

And in Regions farre
Such Heroes bring yee foorth,
As those from whom We came,
And plant Our name,
Vnder that Starre

Not knowne unto our North.

And as there Plenty growes
Of Lawrell every where,
APOLLO'S Sacred tree,
You may it see,
A Poets Browes
To crowne, that may sing there.

Thy Voyages attend,
Industrious HACKLVIT,
Whose Reading shall inflame
Men to seeke Fame,
And much commend
To after-Times thy Wit.

AN ODE WRITTEN IN THE PEAKE

This while we are abroad,
Shall we not touch our Lyre?
Shall we not sing an ODE?
Shall that holy Fire,
In us that strongly glow'd,
In this cold Ayre expire?

Long since the Summer layd
Her lustie Brau'rie downe,
The Autumne halfe is way'd,
And BOREAS 'gins to frowne,
Since now I did behold
Great BRUTES first builded Towne.

Though in the vtmost Peake,
A while we doe remaine,
Amongst the Mountaines bleake
Expos'd to Sleet and Raine,
No Sport our Houres shall breake,
To exercise our Vaine.

What though bright PHŒBUS Beames
Refresh the Southerne Ground,
And though the Princely Thames
With beautious Nymphs abound,
And by old Camber's Streames
Be many Wonders found;

Yet many Rivers cleare
Here glide in Siluer Swathes,
And what of all most deare,
Buckston's delicious Bathes,
Strong Ale and Noble Cheare,
T' asswage breeme Winters scathes.

Those grim and horrid Caves,
Whose Lookes affright the day,
Wherein nice Nature saves,
What she would not bewray,
Our better leasure craves,
And doth invite our Lay.

In places farre or neere,
Or famous, or obscure,
Where wholesome is the Ayre,
Or where the most impure,
All times, and every-where,
The Muse is still in vre.

HIS DEFENCE AGAINST THE IDLE CRITICK

The Ryme nor marres, nor makes,
Nor addeth it, nor takes,
From that which we propose;
Things imaginarie
Doe so strangely varie,
That quickly we them lose.

And what 's quickly begot,
As soone againe is not,
This doe I truely know:
Yea, and what 's borne with paine,
That Sense doth long'st retaine,
Gone with a greater Flow.

Yet this Critick so sterne,
But whom, none must discerne,
Nor perfectly have seeing,
Strangely layes about him,
As nothing without him
Were worthy of being.

That I my selfe betray
To that most publique way,

Where the Worlds old Bawd,
Custome, that doth humor,
And by idle rumor,
Her Dotages applaud.

That whilst he still prefers
Those that be wholly hers,
Madnesse and Ignorance,
I creepe behind the Time,
From spertling with their Crime,
And glad too with my Chance.

O wretched World the while,
When the euill most vile,
Beareth the fayrest face,
And inconstant lightnesse,
With a scornefull slightnesse,
The best Things doth disgrace.

Whilst this strange knowing Beast,
Man, of himselfe the least,
His Enuie declaring,
Makes Vertue to descend,
Her title to defend,
Against him, much preparing.

Yet these me not delude,
Nor from my place extrude,
By their resolued Hate;
Their vilenesse that doe know;
Which to my selfe I show,
To keepe aboue my Fate.

TO HIS RIVALL

Her lov'd I most,
By thee that 's lost,
Though she were wonne with leasure;
She was my gaine,
But to my paine,
Thou spoyl'st me of my Treasure.

The Ship full fraught
With Gold, farre sought,
Though ne'r so wisely helmed,
May suffer wracke

In sayling backe,
By Tempest ouer-whelmed.

But shee, good Sir,
Did not preferre
You, for that I was ranging;
But for that shee
Found faith in mee,
And she lov'd to be changing.

Therefore boast not
Your happy Lot,
Be silent now you have her;
The time I knew
She slighted you,
When I was in her favour.

None stands so fast,
But may be cast
By Fortune, and disgraced:
Once did I weare
Her Garter there,
Where you her Glove have placed.

I had the Vow
That thou hast now,
And Glances to discover
Her Love to mee,
And she to thee
Reades but old Lessons over.

She hath no Smile
That can beguile,
But as my Thought I know it;
Yea, to a Hayre,
Both when and where,
And how she will bestow it.

What now is thine,
Was onely mine,
And first to me was given;
Thou laugh'st at mee,
I laugh at thee,
And thus we two are euen.

But Ile not mourne,
But stay my Turne,
The Wind may come about, Sir,

And once againe
May bring me in,
And help to beare you out, Sir.

The Muse should be sprightly,
Yet not handling lightly
Things grave; as much loath,
Things that be slight, to cloath
Curiously: To retayne
The Comelinesse in meane,
Is true Knowledge and Wit.
Not me forc'd Rage doth fit,
That I thereto should lacke
Tabacco, or need Sacke,
Which to the colder Braine
Is the true Hyppocrene;
Nor did I ever care
For great Fooles, nor them spare.
Vertue, though neglected,
Is not so deiected,
As vilely to descend
To low Basenesse their end;
Neyther each ryming Slave
Deserves the Name to have
Of Poet: so the Rabble
Of Fooles, for the Table,
That have their Iests by Heart,
As an Actor his Part,
Might assume them Chayres
Amongst the Muses Heyres.
Parnassus is not clome
By every such Mome;
Up whose steep side who swerves,
It behoves t' have strong Nerves:
My Resolution such,
How well, and not how much
To write, thus doe I fare,
Like some few good that care
(The evill sort among)
How well to live, and not how long.

Good Folke, for Gold or Hyre,
But helpe me to a Cryer;
For my poore Heart is runne astray
After two Eyes, that pass'd this way.
O yes, O yes, O yes,
If there be any Man,
In Towne or Countrey, can
Bring me my Heart againe,
Ile please him for his paine;
And by these Marks I will you show,
That onely I this Heart doe owe.
It is a wounded Heart,
Wherein yet sticks the Dart,
Ev'ry piece sore hurt throughout it,
Faith, and Troth, writ round about it:
It was a tame Heart, and a deare,
And never us'd to roame;
But hauing got this Haunt, I feare
'Twill hardly stay at home.
For Gods sake, walking by the way,
If you my Heart doe see,
Either impound it for a Stray,
Or send it backe to me.

TO HIS COY LOVE

A CANZONET

I pray thee leave, love me no more,
Call home the Heart you gave me,
I but in vaine that Saint adore,
That can, but will not save me:
These poore halfe Kisses kill me quite;
Was ever man thus served?
Amidst an Ocean of Delight,
For Pleasure to be sterued.

Shew me no more those Snowie Brests,
With Azure Riverets branched,
Where whilst mine Eye with Plentie feasts,
Yet is my Thirst not stanched.
O TANTALUS, thy Paines n'er tell,
By me thou art prevented;
'Tis nothing to be plagu'd in Hell,
But thus in Heaven tormented.

Clip me no more in those deare Armes,
Nor thy Life's Comfort call me;
O, these are but too pow'rfull Charmes,
And doe but more inthrall me.
But see, how patient I am growne,
In all this coyle about thee;
Come nice thing, let my Heart alone,
I cannot live without thee.

A HYMNE TO HIS LADIES BIRTH-PLACE

Couentry, that do'st adorne
The Countrey wherein I was borne,
Yet therein lyes not thy prayse
Why I should crowne thy Tow'rs with Bayes:
'Tis not thy Wall, me to thee weds
Thy Ports, nor thy proud Pyrameds,
Nor thy Trophies of the Bore,
But that Shee which I adore,
Which scarce Goodnesse selfe can payre,
First their breathing blest thy Ayre;
IDEA, in which Name I hide
Her, in my heart Deifi'd,
For what good, Man's mind can see,
Onely her IDEAS be;
She, in whom the Vertues came
In Womans shape, and tooke her Name,
She so farre past Imitation,
As but Nature our Creation
Could not alter, she had aymed,
More then Woman to have framed:
She, whose truely written Story,
To thy poore Name shall adde more glory,
Then if it should have beene thy Chance,
T' have bred our Kings that Conquer'd France.
Had She beene borne the former Age,
That house had beene a Pilgrimage,
And reputed more Diuine,
Then Walsingham or BECKETS Shrine.
That Princesse, to whom thou do'st owe
Thy Freedome, whose Cleere blushing snow,
The envious Sunne saw, when as she
Naked rode to make Thee free,
Was but her Type, as to foretell,
Thou should'st bring forth one, should excell

Her Bounty, by whom thou should'st have
More Honour, then she Freedome gave;
And that great Queene, which but of late
Rul'd this Land in Peace and State,
Had not beene, but Heaven had sworne,
A Maide should raigne, when she was borne.
Of thy Streets, which thou hold'st best,
And most frequent of the rest,
Happy Mich-Parke eu'ry yeere,
On the fourth of August there,
Let thy Maides from FLORA'S bowers,
With their Choyce and daintiest flowers
Decke Thee up, and from their store,
With brave Garlands crowne that dore.
The old Man passing by that way,
To his Sonne in time shall say,
There was that Lady borne, which long
To after-Ages shall be sung;
Who unawares being passed by,
Back to that House shall cast his Eye,
Speaking my Verses as he goes,
And with a Sigh shut eu'ry Close.
Deare Citie, travelling by thee,
When thy rising Spyres I see,
Destined her place of Birth;
Yet me thinkes the very Earth
Hallowed is, so farre as I
Can thee possibly descry:
Then thou dwelling in this place,
Hearing some rude Hinde disgrace
Thy Citie with some scuruy thing,
Which some Iester forth did bring,
Speake these Lines where thou do'st come,
And strike the Slave for ever dumbe.

TO THE CAMBRO-BRITANS AND THEIR HARPE, HIS BALLAD OF AGINCOURT

Faire stood the Wind for France,
When we our Sayles advance,
Nor now to prove our chance,
Longer will tarry;
But putting to the Mayne,
At Kaux, the Mouth of Sene,
With all his Martiall Trayne,
Landed King HARRY.

And taking many a Fort,
Furnish'd in Warlike sort,
Marcheth tow'rds Agincourt,
In happy howre;
Skirmishing day by day,
With those that stop'd his way,
Where the French Gen'rall lay,
With all his Power.

Which in his Hight of Pride,
King HENRY to deride,
His Ransome to provide
To the King sending.
Which he neglects the while,
As from a Nation vile,
Yet with an angry smile,
Their fall portending.

And turning to his Men,
Quoth our brave HENRY then,
Though they to one be ten,
Be not amazed.
Yet have we well begunne,
Battels so bravely wonne,
Have ever to the Sonne,
By Fame beene raysed.

And, for my Selfe (quoth he),
This my full rest shall be,
England ne'r mourne for Me,
Nor more esteeme me.
Victor I will remaine,
Or on this Earth lie slaine,
Never shall Shee sustaine,
Losse to redeeme me.

Poiters and Cressy tell,
When most their Pride did swell,
Under our Swords they fell,
No lesse our skill is,
Than when our Grandsire Great,
Clayming the Regall Seate,
By many a Warlike feate,
Lop'd the French Lillies.

The Duke of Yorke so dread,
The eager Vaward led;
With the maine, HENRY sped,

Among'st his Hench-men.
EXCESTER had the Rere,
A Braver man not there,
O Lord, how hot they were,
On the false French-men!

They now to fight are gone,
Armour on Armour shone,
Drumme now to Drumme did grone,
To heare, was wonder;
That with the Cryes they make,
The very Earth did shake,
Trumpet to Trumpet spake,
Thunder to Thunder.

Well it thine Age became,
O Noble ERPINGHAM,
Which didst the Signall ayme,
To our hid Forces;
When from a Medow by,
Like a Storme suddenly,
The English Archery
Stuck the French Horses,

With Spanish Ewgh so strong,
Arrowes a Cloth-yard long,
That like to Serpents stung,
Piercing the Weather;
None from his fellow starts,
But playing Manly parts,
And like true English hearts,
Stuck close together.

When downe their Bowes they threw,
And forth their Bilbowes drew,
And on the French they flew,
Not one was tardie;
Armes were from shoulders sent,
Scalpes to the Teeth were rent,
Downe the French Pesants went,
Our Men were hardie.

This while our Noble King,
His broad Sword brandishing,
Downe the French Hoast did ding,
As to o'r-whelme it;
And many a deepe Wound lent,
His Armes with Bloud besprent,

And many a cruell Dent
Bruised his Helmet.

GLOSTER, that Duke so good,
Next of the Royall Blood,
For famous England stood,
With his brave Brother;
CLARENCE, in Steele so bright,
Though but a Maiden Knight,
Yet in that furious Fight,
Scarce such another,

WARWICK in Bloud did wade,
OXFORD the Foe invade,
And cruell slaughter made,
Still as they ran up;
SUFFOLKE his Axe did ply,
BEAUMONT and WILLOUGHBY
Bare them right doughtily,
FERRERS and FANHOPE.

Upon Saint CRISPIN'S day
Fought was this Noble Fray,
Which Fame did not delay,
To England to carry;
O, when shall English Men
With such Acts fill a Pen,
Or England breed againe,
Such a King HARRY?

ODE IV

TO MY WORTHY FRIEND, MASTER JOHN SAUAGE OF THE INNER TEMPLE

Upon this sinfull earth
If man can happy be,
And higher then his birth,
(Frend) take him thus from me.

Whome promise not deceives
That he the breach should rue,
Nor constant reason leaves
Opinion to pursue.

To rayse his mean estate
That sooths no wanton's sinne,

Doth that preferment hate
That virtue doth not winne.

Nor bravery doth admire,
Nor doth more love professe
To that he doth desire,
Then that he doth possesse.

Loose humor nor to please,
That neither spares nor spends,
But by discretion weyes
What is to needfull ends.

To him deseruing not
Not yeelding, nor doth hould
What is not his, doing what
He ought not what he could.

Whome the base tyrants will
Soe much could never awe
As him for good or ill
From honesty to drawe.

Whose constancy doth rise
'Boue undeserued spight
Whose valewr's to despise
That most doth him delight.

That earely leave doth take
Of th' world though to his payne
For virtues onely sake
And not till need constrayne.

Noe man can be so free
Though in imperiall seate
Nor Eminent as he
That deemeth nothing greate.

ODE VIII

Singe wee the Rose
Then which no flower there growes
Is sweeter:
And aptly her compare
With what in that is rare
A parallel none meeter.

Or made poses,
Of this that incloses
Suche blisses,
That naturally flusheth
As she blusheth
When she is robd of kisses.

Or if strew'd
When with the morning dew'd
Or stilling,
Or howe to sense expos'd
All which in her inclos'd,
Ech place with sweetnes filling.

That most renown'd
By Nature richly crownd
With yellow,
Of that delitious layre
And as pure, her hayre
Vnto the same the fellowe,

Fearing of harme
Nature that flower doth arme
From danger,
The touch giues her offence
But with reverence
Vnto her selfe a stranger.

That redde, or white,
Or mixt, the sence delyte
Behoulding,
In her complexion
All which perfection
Such harmony infouldinge.

That deuyded
Ere it was descided
Which most pure,
Began the greeuous war
Of York and Lancaster,
That did many yeeres indure.

Conflicts as greate
As were in all that heate
I sustaine:
By her, as many harts
As men on either parts

That with her eies hath slaine.

The Primrose flower
The first of Flora's bower
Is placed,
Soo is shee first as best
Though excellent the rest,
All gracing, by none graced.

ELEGIES UPON SUNDRY OCCASIONS

OF HIS LADIES NOT COMING TO LONDON

That ten-yeares-travell'd Greeke return'd from Sea
Ne'r joyd so much to see his Ithaca,
As I should you, who are alone to me,
More then wide Greece could to that wanderer be.
The winter windes still Easterly doe keepe,
And with keene Frosts have chained up the deepe,
The Sunne's to us a niggard of his Rayes,
But reVelleth with our Antipodes;
And seldome to us when he shewes his head,
Muffled in vapours, he straight hies to bed.
In those bleake mountaines can you liue where snowe
Maketh the vales up to the hilles to growe;
Whereas mens breathes doe instantly congeale,
And attom'd mists turne instantly to hayle;
Belike you thinke, from this more temperate cost,
My sighes may haVe the power to thawe the frost,
Which I from hence should swiftly send you thither,
Yet not so swift, as you come slowly hither.
How many a time, hath Phebe from her wayne,
With Phœbus fires fill'd up her hornes againe;
Shee through her Orbe, still on her course doth range,
But you keep yours still, nor for me will change.
The Sunne that mounted the sterne Lions back,
Shall with the Fishes shortly diue the Brack,
But still you keepe your station, which confines
You, nor regard him travelling the signes.
Those ships which when you went, put out to Sea,
Both to our Groenland, and Virginia,
Are now return'd, and Custom'd have their fraught,
Yet you arriue not, nor returne me ought.
The Thames was not so frozen yet this yeare,
As is my bosome, with the chilly feare
Of your not comming, which on me doth light,

As on those Climes, where halfe the world is night.
Of every tedious houre you have made two,
All this long Winter here, by missing you:
Minutes are months, and when the houre is past,
A yeare is ended since the Clocke strooke last,
When your Remembrance puts me on the Racke,
And I should Swound to see an Almanacke,
To reade what silent weekes away are slid,
Since the dire Fates you from my sight have hid.
I hate him who the first Deuisor was
Of this same foolish thing, the Hower-glasse,
And of the Watch, whose dribbling sands and Wheele,
With their slow stroakes, make mee too much to feele
Your slackenesse hither, O how I doe ban,
Him that these Dialls against walles began,
Whose Snayly motion of the moouing hand,
(Although it goe) yet seeme to me to stand;
As though at Adam it had first set out
And had been stealing all this while about,
And when it backe to the first point should come,
It shall be then just at the generall Doome.
The Seas into themselues retract their flowes.
The changing Winde from every quarter blowes,
Declining Winter in the Spring doth call,
The Starrs rise to us, as from us they fall;
Those Birdes we see, that leave us in the Prime,
Againe in Autumne re-salute our Clime.
Sure, either Nature you from kinde hath made,
Or you delight else to be Retrograde.
But I perceiue by your attractiue powers,
Like an Inchantresse you have charm'd the bowers
Into short minutes, and have drawne them back,
So that of us at London, you doe lack
Almost a yeare, the Spring is scarce begonne
There where you liue, and Autumne almost done.
With us more Eastward, surely you deuise,
By your strong Magicke, that the Sunne shall rise
Where now it setts, and that in some few yeares
You'l alter quite the Motion of the Spheares.
Yes, and you meane, I shall complaine my love
To gravell'd Walkes, or to a stupid Groue,
Now your companions; and that you the while
(As you are cruell) will sit by and smile,
To make me write to these, while Passers by,
Sleightly looke in your lovely face, where I
See Beauties heaven, whilst silly blockheads, they
Like laden Asses, plod upon their way,
And wonder not, as you should point a Clowne

Vp to the Guards, or Ariadnes Crowne;
Of Constellations, and his dulnesse tell.
Hee'd thinke your words were certainly a Spell;
Or him some piece from Creet, or Marcus show,
In all his life which till that time ne'r saw
Painting: except in Alehouse or old Hall
Done by some Druzzler, of the Prodigall.
Nay doe, stay still, whilst time away shall steale
Your youth, and beautie, and your selfe conceale
From me I pray you, you have now inur'd
Me to your absence, and I have endur'd
Your want this long, whilst I have starued bine
For your short Letters, as you helde it sinne
To write to me, that to appease my woe,
I reade ore those, you writ a yeare agoe,
Which are to me, as though they had bin made,
Long time before the first Olympiad.
For thankes and curt'sies sell your presence then
To tatling Women, and to things like men,
And be more foolish then the Indians are
For Bells, for Kniues, for Glasses, and such ware,
That sell their Pearle and Gold, but here I stay,
So I would not have you but come away.

TO MASTER GEORGE SANDYS

Treasurer for the English Colony in Virginia

Friend, if you thinke my Papers may supplie
You, with some strange omitted Noveltie,
Which others Letters yet have left untould,
You take me off, before I can take hould
Of you at all; I put not thus to Sea,
For two monthes Voyage to Virginia,
With newes which now, a little something here,
But will be nothing ere it can come there.
I feare, as I doe Stabbing; this word, State,
I dare not speake of the Palatinate,
Although some men make it their hourely theame,
And talke what's done in Austria, and in Beame,
I may not so; what Spinola intends,
Nor with his Dutch, which way Prince Maurice bends;
To other men, although these things be free,
Yet (GEORGE) they must be misteries to mee.
I scarce dare praise a vertuous friend that's dead,
Lest for my lines he should be censured;

It was my hap before all other men
To suffer shipwrack by my forward pen:
When King JAMES entred; at which joyfull time
I taught his title to this Ile in rime:
And to my part did all the Muses win,
With high-pitch Pæans to applaud him in:
When cowardise had tyed up every tongue,
And all stood silent, yet for him I sung;
And when before by danger I was dar'd,
I kick'd her from me, nor a iot I spar'd.
Yet had not my cleere spirit in Fortunes scorne,
Me aboue earth and her afflictions borne;
He next my God on whom I built my trust,
Had left me troden lower then the dust:
But let this passe; in the extreamest ill,
Apollo's brood must be couragious still,
Let Pies, and Dawes, sit dumb before their death,
Onely the Swan sings at the parting breath.
And (worthy GEORGE) by industry and use,
Let's see what lines Virginia will produce;
Goe on with OVID, as you have begunne,
With the first fiue Bookes; let your numbers run
Glib as the former, so shall it liue long,
And doe much honour to the English tongue:
Intice the Muses thither to repaire,
Intreat them gently, trayne them to that ayre,
For they from hence may thither hap to fly,
T'wards the sad time which but to fast doth hie,
For Poesie is follow'd with such spight,
By groueling drones that never raught her height,
That she must hence, she may no longer staye:
The driery fates prefixed have the day,
Of her departure, which is now come on,
And they command her straight wayes to be gon;
That bestiall heard so hotly her pursue,
And to her succour, there be very few,
Nay none at all, her wrongs that will redresse,
But she must wander in the wildernesse,
Like to the woman, which that holy JOHN
Beheld in Pathmos in his vision.
As th' English now, so did the stiff-neckt Iewes,
Their noble Prophets vtterly refuse,
And of these men such poore opinions had;
They counted Esay and Ezechiel mad;
When Jeremy his Lamentations writ,
They thought the Wizard quite out of his wit,
Such sots they were, as worthily to ly,
Lock't in the chaines of their captiuity,

Knowledge hath still her Eddy in her Flow,
So it hath beene, and it will still be so.
That famous Greece where learning flourisht most,
Hath of her muses long since left to boast,
Th' unlettered Turke, and rude Barbarian trades,
Where HOMER sang his lofty Iliads;
And this vaste volume of the world hath taught,
Much may to passe in little time be brought.
As if to Symptoms we may credit giue,
This very time, wherein we two now liue,
Shall in the compasse, wound the Muses more,
Then all the old English ignorance before;
Base Balatry is so belov'd and sought,
And those brave numbers are put by for naught,
Which rarely read, were able to awake,
Bodyes from graves, and to the ground to shake
The wandring clouds, and to our men at armes,
'Gainst pikes and muskets were most powerfull charmes.
That, but I know, insuing ages shall,
Raise her againe, who now is in her fall;
And out of dust reduce our scattered rimes,
Th' reiected iewels of these slothfull times,
Who with the Muses would misspend an hower,
But let blind Gothish Barbarisme deuoure
These feverous Dogdays, blest by no record,
But to be everlastingly abhord.
If you vouchsafe rescription, stuffe your quill
With naturall bountyes, and impart your skill,
In the description of the place, that I,
May become learned in the soyle thereby;
Of noble Wyats health, and let me heare,
The Governour; and how our people there,
Increase and labour, what supplyes are sent,
Which I confesse shall giue me much content;
But you may save your labour if you please,
To write to me ought of your Sauages.
As sauage slaves be in great Britaine here,
As any one that you can shew me there
And though for this, Ile say I doe not thirst,
Yet I should like it well to be the first,
Whose numbers hence into Virginia flew,
So (noble Sandis) for this time adue.

TO MY NOBLE FRIEND MASTER WILLIAM BROWNE, OF THE EVIL TIME

Deare friend, be silent and with patience see,

What this mad times Catastrophe will be;
The worlds first Wisemen certainly mistooke
Themselves, and spoke things quite beside the booke,
And that which they have of said of God, untrue,
Or else expect strange judgement to insue.
This Isle is a meere Bedlam, and therein,
We all lye raving, mad in every sinne,
And him the wisest most men use to call,
Who doth (alone) the maddest thing of all;
He whom the master of all wisedome found,
For a marckt foole, and so did him propound,
The time we liue in, to that passe is brought,
That only he a Censor now is thought;
And that base villaine, (not an age yet gone,)
Which a good man would not have look'd upon;
Now like a God, with diuine worship follow'd,
And all his actions are accounted hollow'd.
This world of ours, thus runneth upon wheeles,
Set on the head, bolt upright with her heeles;
Which makes me thinke of what the Ethnicks told
Th' opinion, the Pythagorists uphold,
That the immortall soule doth transmigrate;
Then I suppose by the strong power of fate,
And since that time now many a lingering yeare,
Through fools, and beasts, and lunatiques have past,
Are heere imbodyed in this age at last,
And though so long we from that time be gone,
Yet taste we still of that confusion.
For certainely there's scarse one found that now,
Knowes what t' approoue, or what to disallow,
All arsey varsey, nothing is it's owne,
But to our prouerbe, all turnd upside downe;
To doe in time, is to doe out of season,
And that speeds best, thats done the farth'st from reason,
Hee 's high'st that 's low'st, hee 's surest in that 's out,
He hits the next way that goes farth'st about,
He getteth up unlike to rise at all,
He slips to ground as much unlike to fall;
Which doth inforce me partly to prefer,
The opinion of that mad Philosopher,
Who taught, that those all-framing powers above,
(As 'tis suppos'd) made man not out of love
To him at all, but only as a thing,
To make them sport with, which they use to bring
As men doe munkeys, puppets, and such tooles
Of laughter: so men are but the Gods fooles.
Such are by titles lifted to the sky,
As wherefore no man knowes, God scarcely why;

The vertuous man depressed like a stone,
For that dull Sot to raise himselfe upon;
He who ne're thing yet worthy man durst doe,
Never durst looke upon his countrey's foe,
Nor durst attempt that action which might get
Him fame with men: or higher might him set
Then the base begger (rightly if compar'd;)
This Drone yet never brave attempt that dar'd,
Yet dares be knighted, and from thence dares grow
To any title Empire can bestow;
For this beleeue, that Impudence is now
A Cardinall vertue, and men it allow
Reverence, nay more, men study and inuent
New wayes, nay, glory to be impudent.
Into the clouds the Deuill lately got,
And by the moisture doubting much the rot,
A medicine tooke to make him purge and cast;
Which in short time began to worke so fast,
That he fell too 't, and from his backeside flew,
A rout of rascall a rude ribauld crew
Of base Plebeians, which no sooner light,
Vpon the earth, but with a suddaine flight,
They spread this Ile, and as Deucalion once
Ouer his shoulder backe, by throwing stones
They became men, euen so these beasts became,
Owners of titles from an obscure name.
He that by riot, of a mighty rent,
Hath his late goodly Patrimony spent,
And into base and wilfull beggery run
This man as he some glorious acte had done,
With some great pension, or rich guift releeu'd,
When he that hath by industry atchieu'd
Some noble thing, contemned and disgrac'd,
In the forlorne hope of the times is plac'd,
As though that God had carelessely left all
That being hath on this terrestriall ball,
To fortunes guiding, nor would have to doe
With man, nor aught that doth belong him to,
Or at the least God hauing giuen more
Power to the Deuill, then he did of yore,
Ouer this world: the feind as he doth hate
The vertuous man; maligning his estate,
All noble things, and would have by his will,
To be damn'd with him, using all his skill,
By his blacke hellish ministers to vexe
All worthy men, and strangely to perplexe
Their constancie, there by them so to fright,
That they should yeeld them wholely to his might.

But of these things I vainely doe but tell,
Where hell is heaven, and heav'n is now turn'd hell;
Where that which lately blasphemy hath bin,
Now godlinesse, much lesse accounted sin;
And a long while I greatly meruail'd why
Buffoons and Bawdes should hourely multiply,
Till that of late I construed it that they
To present thrift had got the perfect way,
When I concluded by their odious crimes,
It was for us no thriuing in these times.
As men oft laugh at little Babes, when they
Hap to behold some strange thing in their play,
To see them on the suddaine strucken sad,
As in their fancie some strange formes they had,
Which they by pointing with their fingers showe,
Angry at our capacities so slowe,
That by their countenance we no sooner learne
To see the wonder which they so discerne:
So the celestiall powers doe sit and smile
At innocent and vertuous men the while,
They stand amazed at the world ore-gone,
So farre beyond imagination,
With slauish basenesse, that the silent sit
Pointing like children in describing it.
Then noble friend the next way to controule
These worldly crosses, is to arme thy soule
With constant patience: and with thoughts as high
As these be lowe, and poore, winged to flye
To that exalted stand, whether yet they
Are got with paine, that sit out of the way
Of this ignoble age, which raiseth none
But such as thinke their black damnation
To be a trifle; such, so ill, that when
They are aduanc'd, those few poore honest men
That yet are liuing, into search doe runne
To finde what mischiefe they have lately done,
Which so preferres them; say thou he doth rise,
That maketh vertue his chiefe exercise.
And in this base world come what ever shall,
Hees worth lamenting, that for her doth fall.

UPON THE THREE SONNES OF THE LORD SHEFFIELD, DROWNED IN HUMBER

Light Sonnets hence, and to loose Lovers flie,
And mournfull Maydens sing an Elegie
On those three SHEFFIELDS, ouer-whelm'd with waves,

Whose losse the teares of all the Muses craves;
A thing so full of pitty as this was,
Me thinkes for nothing should not slightly passe.
Treble this losse was, why should it not borrowe,
Through this Iles treble parts, a treble sorrowe:
But Fate did this, to let the world to knowe,
That sorrowes which from common causes growe,
Are not worth mourning for, the losse to beare,
But of one onely sonne, 's not worth one teare.
Some tender-hearted man, as I, may spend
Some drops (perhaps) for a deceased friend.
Some men (perhaps) their Wifes late death may rue;
Or Wifes their Husbands, but such be but fewe.
Cares that have us'd the hearts of men to tuch
So oft, and deepely, will not now be such;
Who'll care for loss of maintenance, or place,
Fame, liberty, or of the Princes grace;
Or sutes in law, by base corruption crost,
When he shall finde, that this which he hath lost,
Alas, is nothing to his, which did lose,
Three sonnes at once so excellent as those:
Nay, it is feard that this in time may breed
Hard hearts in men to their owne naturall seed;
That in respect of this great losse of theirs,
Men will scarce mourne the death of their owne heires.
Through all this Ile their losse so publique is,
That every man doth take them to be his,
And as a plague which had beginning there,
So catching is, and raigning every where,
That those the farthest off as much doe rue them,
As those the most familiarly that knew them;
Children with this disaster are wext sage,
And like to men that strucken are in age;
Talke what it is, three children at one time
Thus to have drown'd, and in their very prime;
Yea, and doe learne to act the same so well,
That then olde folke, they better can it tell.
Inuention, oft that Passion us'd to faine,
In sorrowes of themselves but slight, and meane,
To make them seeme great, here it shall not need,
For that this Subiect doth so farre exceed
All forc'd Expression, that what Poesie shall
Happily thinke to grace it selfe withall,
Falls so belowe it, that it rather borrowes
Grace from their griefe, then addeth to their sorrowes,
For sad mischance thus in the losse of three,
To shewe it selfe the vtmost it could bee:
Exacting also by the selfe same lawe,

The vtmost teares that sorrowe had to drawe
All future times hath vtterly preuented
Of a more losse, or more to be lamented.
Whilst in faire youth they liuely flourish'd here,
To their kinde Parents they were onely deere:
But being dead, now every one doth take
Them for their owne, and doe like sorrowe make:
As for their owne begot, as they pretended
Hope in the issue, which should have discended
From them againe; nor here doth end our sorrow,
But those of us, that shall be borne to morrowe
Still shall lament them, and when time shall count,
To what vast number passed yeares shall mount,
They from their death shall duly reckon so,
As from the Deluge, former us'd to doe.
O cruell Humber guilty of their gore,
I now beleeue more then I did before
The Brittish Story, whence thy name begun
Of Kingly Humber, an inuading Hun,
By thee deuoured, for't is likely thou
With blood wert Christned, bloud-thirsty till now.
The Ouse, the Done, and thou farre clearer Trent,
To drowne the SHEFFIELDS as you gave consent,
Shall curse the time, that ere you were infus'd,
Which have your waters basely thus abus'd.
The groueling Boore yee hinder not to goe,
And at his pleasure Ferry to and fro.
The very best part of whose soule, and bloud,
Compared with theirs, is viler then your mud.
But wherefore paper, doe I idely spend,
On those deafe waters to so little end,
And up to starry heaven doe I not looke,
In which, as in an everlasting booke,
Our ends are written; O let times rehearse
Their fatall losse, in their sad Aniuerse.

TO THE NOBLE LADY, THE LADY I.S. OF WORLDLY CROSSES

Madame, to shew the smoothnesse of my vaine,
Neither that I would have you entertaine
The time in reading me, which you would spend
In faire discourse with some knowne honest friend,
I write not to you. Nay, and which is more,
My powerfull verses strive not to restore,
What time and sicknesse have in you impair'd,
To other ends my Elegie is squar'd.

Your beauty, sweetnesse, and your gracefull parts
That have drawne many eyes, wonne many hearts,
Of me get little, I am so much man,
That let them doe their utmost that they can,
I will resist their forces: and they be
Though great to others, yet not so to me.
The first time I beheld you, I then sawe
That (in it selfe) which had the power to drawe
My stayd affection, and thought to allowe
You some deale of my heart; but you have now
Got farre into it, and you have the skill
(For ought I see) to winne upon me still.
When I doe thinke how bravely you have borne
Your many crosses, as in Fortunes scorne,
And how neglectfull you have seem'd to be,
Of that which hath seem'd terrible to me,
I thought you stupid, nor that you had felt
Those griefes which (often) I have scene to melt
Another woman into sighes and teares,
A thing but seldome in your sexe and yeares,
But when in you I have perceiu'd agen,
(Noted by me, more then by other men)
How feeling and how sensible you are
Of your friends sorrowes, and with how much care
You seeke to cure them, then my selfe I blame,
That I your patience should so much misname,
Which to my understanding maketh knowne
Who feeles anothers griefe, can feele their owne.
When straight me thinkes, I heare your patience say,
Are you the man that studied Seneca:
Plinies most learned letters; and must I
Read you a Lecture in Philosophie,
T'auoid the afflictions that have us'd to reach you;
I'le learne you more, Sir, then your bookes can teach you.
Of all your sex, yet never did I knowe,
Any that yet so actually could showe
Such rules for patience, such an easie way,
That who so sees it, shall be forc'd to say,
Loe what before seem'd hard to be discern'd,
Is of this Lady, in an instant learn'd.
It is heavens will that you should wronged be
By the malicious, that the world might see
Your Doue-like meekenesse; for had the base scumme,
The spawne of Fiends, beene in your slander dumbe,
Your vertue then had perish'd, never priz'd,
For that the same you had not exercised;
And you had lost the Crowne you have, and glory,
Nor had you beene the subiect of my Story.

Whilst they feele Hell, being damned in their hate,
Their thoughts like Deuils them excruciate,
Which by your noble suffrings doe torment
Them with new paines, and giues you this content
To see your soule an Innocent, hath suffred,
And up to heaven before your eyes be offred:
Your like we in a burning Glasse may see,
When the Sunnes rayes therein contracted be
Bent on some obiect, which is purely white,
We finde that colour doth dispierce the light,
And stands untainted: but if it hath got
Some little sully; or the least small spot,
Then it soon fiers it; so you still remaine
Free, because in you they can finde no staine.
God doth not love them least, on whom he layes
The great'st afflictions; but that he will praise
Himselfe most in them, and will make them fit,
Near'st to himselfe who is the Lambe to sit:
For by that touch, like perfect gold he tries them,
Who are not his, untill the world denies them.
And your example may work such effect,
That it may be the beginning of a Sect
Of patient women; and that many a day
All Husbands may for you their Founder pray.
Nor is to me your Innocence the lesse,
In that I see you striue not to suppresse
Their barbarous malice; but your noble heart
Prepar'd to act so difficult a part,
With unremoued constancie is still
The same it was, that of your proper ill,
The effect proceeds from your owne selfe the cause,
Like some just Prince, who to establish lawes,
Suffers the breach at his best lov'd to strike,
To learne the vulgar to endure the like.
You are a Martir thus, nor can you be
Lesse to the world so valued by me:
If as you have begun, you still persever
Be ever good, that I may love you ever.

AN ELEGIE UPON THE DEATH OF THE LADY PENELOPE CLIFTON

Must I needes write, who's hee that can refuse,
He wants a minde, for her that hath no Muse,
The thought of her doth heav'nly rage inspire,
Next powerfull, to those cloven tongues of fire.
Since I knew ought time never did allowe

Me stuffe fit for an Elegie, till now;
When France and England's HENRIES dy'd, my quill,
Why, I know not, but it that time lay still.
'Tis more then greatnesse that my spirit must raise,
To observe custome I use not to praise;
Nor the least thought of mine yet ere depended,
On any one from whom she was descended;
That for their fauour I this way should wooe,
As some poor wretched things (perhaps) may doe;
I gaine the end, whereat I onely ayme,
If by my freedome, I may giue her fame.
Walking then forth being newly up from bed,
O Sir (quoth one) the Lady CLIFTON'S dead.
When, but that reason my sterne rage withstood,
My hand had sure beene guilty of his blood.
If shee be so, must thy rude tongue confesse it
(Quoth I) and com'st so coldly to expresse it.
Thou shouldst have given a shreeke, to make me feare thee;
That might have slaine what ever had beene neere thee.
Thou shouldst have com'n like Time with thy scalpe bare,
And in thy hands thou shouldst have brought thy haire,
Casting upon me such a dreadfull looke,
As seene a spirit, or th'adst beene thunder-strooke,
And gazing on me so a little space,
Thou shouldst have shot thine eye balls in my face,
Then falling at my feet, thou shouldst have said,
O she is gone, and Nature with her dead.
With this ill newes amaz'd by chance I past,
By that neere Groue, whereas both first and last,
I saw her, not three moneths before shee di'd.
When (though full Summer gan to vaile her pride,
And that I sawe men leade home ripened Corne,
Besides aduis'd me well,) I durst have sworne
The lingring yeare, the Autumne had adiourn'd,
And the fresh Spring had beene againe return'd,
Her delicacie, lovelinesse, and grace,
With such a Summer bravery deckt the place:
But now alas, it lookt forlorne and dead;
And where she stood, the fading leaves were shed,
Presenting onely sorrowe to my sight,
O God (thought I) this is her Embleme right.
And sure I thinke it cannot but be thought,
That I to her by providence was brought.
For that the Fates fore-dooming, shee should die,
Shewed me this wondrous Master peece, that I
Should sing her Funerall, that the world should know it,
That heaven did thinke her worthy of a Poet;
My hand is fatall, nor doth fortune doubt,

For what it writes, not fire shall ere race out.
A thousand silken Puppets should have died,
And in their fulsome Coffins putrified,
Ere in my lines, you of their names should heare
To tell the world that such there ever were,
Whose memory shall from the earth decay,
Before those Rags be worne they gave away:
Had I her god-like features never seene,
Poore slight Report had tolde me she had beene
A hansome Lady, comely, very well,
And so might I have died an Infidell,
As many doe which never did her see,
Or cannot credit, what she was, by mee.
Nature, her selfe, that before Art prefers
To goe beyond all our Cosmographers,
By Charts and Maps exactly that have showne,
All of this earth that ever can be knowne,
For that she would beyond them all descrie
What Art could not by any mortall eye;
A Map of heaven in her rare features drue,
And that she did so liuely and so true,
That any soule but seeing it might sweare
That all was perfect heavenly that was there.
If ever any Painter were so blest,
To drawe that face, which so much heau'n exprest,
If in his best of skill he did her right,
I wish it never may come in my sight,
I greatly doubt my faith (weake man) lest I
Should to that face commit Idolatry.
Death might have tyth'd her sex, but for this one,
Nay, have ta'n halfe to have let her alone;
Such as their wrinkled temples to supply,
Cyment them up with sluttish Mercury,
Such as undrest were able to affright,
A valiant man approching him by night;
Death might have taken such, her end deferd,
Vntill the time she had beene climaterd;
When she would have bin at threescore yeares and three,
Such as our best at three and twenty be,
With enuie then, he might have ouerthrowne her,
When age nor time had power to ceaze upon her.
But when the unpittying Fates her end decreed,
They to the same did instantly proceed,
For well they knew (if she had languish'd so)
As those which hence by naturall causes goe,
So many prayers, and teares for her had spoken,
As certainly their Iron lawes had broken,
And had wak'd heau'n, who clearely would have show'd

That change of Kingdomes to her death it ow'd;
And that the world still of her end might thinke,
It would have let some Neighbouring mountaine sinke.
Or the vast Sea it in on us to cast,
As Severne did about some fiue yeares past:
Or some sterne Comet his curld top to reare,
Whose length should measure halfe our Hemisphere.
Holding this height, to say some will not sticke,
That now I rave, and am growne lunatique:
You of what sexe so ere you be, you lye,
'Tis thou thy selfe is lunatique, not I.
I charge you in her name that now is gone,
That may coniure you, if you be not stone,
That you no harsh, nor shallow rimes decline,
Vpon that day wherein you shall read mine.
Such as indeed are falsely termed verse,
And will but sit like mothes upon her herse;
Nor that no child, nor chambermaide, nor page,
Disturbe the Rome, the whilst my sacred rage,
In reading is; but whilst you heare it read,
Suppose, before you, that you see her dead,
The walls about you hung with mournfull blacke,
And nothing of her funerall to lacke,
And when this period gives you leave to pause,
Cast up your eyes, and sigh for my applause.

UPON THE NOBLE LADY ASTONS DEPARTURE FOR SPAINE

I many a time have greatly marveil'd, why
Men say, their friends depart when as they die,
How well that word, a dying, doth expresse,
I did not know (I freely must confesse,)
Till her departure: for whose missed sight,
I am enforc'd this Elegy to write:
But since resistlesse fate will have it so,
That she from hence must to Iberia goe,
And my weak wishes can her not detaine,
I will of heaven in policy complaine,
That it so long her travell should adiourne,
Hoping thereby to hasten her returne.
Can those of Norway for their wage procure,
By their blacke spells a winde that shall endure
Till from aboard the wished land men see,
And fetch the harbour, where they long to be,
Can they by charmes doe this and cannot I
Who am the Priest of Phœbus, and so hie,

Sit in his favour, winne the Poets god,
To send swift Hermes with his snaky rod,
To Æolus Cave, commanding him with care,
His prosperous winds, that he for her prepare,
And from that howre, wherein shee takes the seas,
Nature bring on the quiet Halcion dayes,
And in that hower that bird begin her nest,
Nay at that very instant, that long rest
May seize on Neptune, who may still repose,
And let that bird nere till that hower disclose,
Wherein she landeth, and for all that space
Be not a wrinkle seene on Thetis face,
Onely so much breath with a gentle gale,
As by the easy swelling of her saile,
May at Sebastians safely set her downe
Where, with her goodnes she may blesse the towne.
If heaven in justice would have plagu'd by thee
Some Pirate, and grimme Neptune thou should'st be
His Executioner, or what is his worse,
The gripple Merchant, borne to be the curse
Of this brave Iland; let them for her sake,
Who to thy safeguard doth her selfe betake,
Escape undrown'd, unwrackt, nay rather let
Them be at ease in some safe harbour set,
Where with much profit they may vent their wealth
That they have got by villany and stealth,
Rather great Neptune, then when thou dost rave,
Thou once shouldst wet her saile but with a wave.
Or if some proling Rouer shall but dare,
To seize the ship wherein she is to fare,
Let the fell fishes of the Maine appeare,
And tell those Sea-thiefes, that once such they were
As they are now, till they assaid to rape
Grape-crowned Bacchus in a striplings shape,
That came aboard them, and would faine have saild,
To vine-spread Naxus but that him they faild,
Which he perceiuing, them so monstrous made,
And warnd them how they passengers inuade.
Ye South and Westerne winds now cease to blow
Autumne is come, there be no flowers to grow,
Yea from that place respire, to which she goes,
And to her sailes should show your selfe but foes,
But Boreas and yee Esterne windes arise,
To send her soon to Spaine, but be precise,
That in your aide you seeme not still so sterne,
As we a summer should no more discerne,
For till that here againe, I may her see,
It will be winter all the yeare with mee.

Ye swanne-begotten lonely brother-stars,
So oft auspicious to poore Mariners,
Ye twin-bred lights of lovely Leda's brood,
Leda in the loues egge-borne issue smile upon the flood,
And in your mild'st aspect doe ye appeare
To be her warrant from all future feare.
And if thou ship that bear'st her, doe prove good,
May never time by wormes, consume thy wood
Nor rust thy iron, may thy tacklings last,
Till they for reliques be in temples plac't;
Maist thou be ranged with that mighty Arke,
Wherein just Noah did all the world imbarque,
With that which after Troyes so famous wracke,
From ten yeares travell brought Ulisses backe,
That Argo which to Colchos went from Greece,
And in her botome brought the goulden fleece
Under brave Jason; or that same of Drake,
Wherein he did his famous voyage make
About the world; or Candishes that went
As far as his, about the Continent.
And yee milde winds that now I doe implore,
Not once to raise the least sand on the shore,
Nor once on forfait of your selues respire:
When once the time is come of her retire,
If then it please you, but to doe your due,
What for these windes I did, Ile doe for you;
Ile wooe you then, and if that not suffice,
My pen shall prooue you to have dietyes,
Ile sing your loves in verses that shall flow,
And tell the storyes of your weale and woe,
Ile prooue what profit to the earth you bring,
And how t'is you that welcome in the spring;
Ile raise up altars to you, as to show,
The time shall be kept holy, when you blow.
O blessed winds! your will that it may be,
To send health to her, and her home to me.

TO MY MOST DEARLY-LOVED FRIEND HENRY REYNOLDS ESQ, OF POETS & POESIE

My dearely loved friend how oft have we,
In winter evenings (meaning to be free,)
To some well-chosen place us'd to retire;
And there with moderate meate, and wine, and fire,
Have past the howres contentedly with chat,
Now talk of this, and then discours'd of that,
Spoke our owne verses 'twixt our selves, if not

Other mens lines, which we by chance had got,
Or some Stage pieces famous long before,
Of which your happy memory had store;
And I remember you much pleased were,
Of those who lived long agoe to heare,
As well as of those, of these latter times,
Who have inricht our language with their rimes,
And in succession, how still up they grew,
Which is the subject, that I now pursue;
For from my cradle, (you must know that) I,
Was still inclin'd to noble Poesie,
And when that once Pueriles I had read,
And newly had my Cato construed,
In my small selfe I greatly marueil'd then,
Amonst all other, what strange kinde of men
These Poets were; And pleased with the name,
To my milde Tutor merrily I came,
(For I was then a proper goodly page,
Much like a Pigmy, scarse ten yeares of age)
Clasping my slender armes about his thigh.
O my deare master! cannot you (quoth I)
Make me a Poet, doe it if you can,
And you shall see, Ile quickly bee a man,
Who me thus answered smiling, boy quoth he,
If you'le not play the wag, but I may see
You ply your learning, I will shortly read
Some Poets to you; Phœbus be my speed,
Too't hard went I, when shortly he began,
And first read to me honest Mantuan,
Then Virgils Eglogues, being entred thus,
Me thought I straight had mounted Pegasus,
And in his full Careere could make him stop,
And bound upon Parnassus' by-clift top.
I scornd your ballet then though it were done
And had for Finis, William Elderton.
But soft, in sporting with this childish iest,
I from my subiect have too long digrest,
Then to the matter that we tooke in hand,
Love and Apollo for the Muses stand.
Then noble Chaucer, in those former times,
The first inrich'd our English with his rimes,
And was the first of ours, that ever brake,
Into the Muses treasure, and first spake
In weighty numbers, deluing in the Mine
Of perfect knowledge, which he could refine,
And coyne for currant, and as much as then
The English language could expresse to men,
He made it doe; and by his wondrous skill,

Gave us much light from his abundant quill.
And honest Gower, who in respect of him,
Had only sipt at Aganippas brimme,
And though in yeares this last was him before,
Yet fell he far short of the others store.
When after those, foure ages very neare,
They with the Muses which conuersed, were
That Princely Surrey, early in the time
Of the Eight Henry, who was then the prime
Of Englands noble youth; with him there came
Wyat; with reuerence whom we still doe name
Amongst our Poets, Brian had a share
With the two former, which accompted are
That times best makers, and the authors were
Of those small poems, which the title beare,
Of songs and sonnets, wherein oft they hit
On many dainty passages of wit.
Gascoine and Churchyard after them againe
In the beginning of Eliza's raine,
Accoumpted were great Meterers many a day,
But not inspired with brave fier, had they
Liu'd but a little longer, they had seene,
Their works before them to have buried beene.
Grave morrall Spencer after these came on
Then whom I am perswaded there was none
Since the blind Bard his Iliads up did make,
Fitter a taske like that to undertake,
To set downe boldly, bravely to inuent,
In all high knowledge, surely excellent.
The noble Sidney with this last arose,
That Heroe for numbers, and for Prose.
That throughly pac'd our language as to show,
The plenteous English hand in hand might goe
With Greek or Latine, and did first reduce
Our tongue from Lillies writing then in use;
Talking of Stones, Stars, Plants, of fishes, Flyes,
Playing with words, and idle Similies,
As th' English, Apes and very Zanies be,
Of every thing, that they doe heare and see,
So imitating his ridiculous tricks,
They spake and writ, all like meere lunatiques.
Then Warner though his lines were not so trim'd,
Nor yet his Poem so exactly lim'd
And neatly joynted, but the Criticke may
Easily reprooue him, yet thus let me say;
For my old friend, some passages there be
In him, which I protest have taken me,
With almost wonder, so fine, cleere, and new

As yet they have bin equalled by few.
Neat Marlow bathed in the Thespian springs
Had in him those brave translunary things,
That the first Poets had, his raptures were,
All ayre, and fire, which made his verses cleere,
For that fine madnes still he did retaine,
Which rightly should possesse a Poets braine.
And surely Nashe, though he a Proser were
A branch of Lawrell yet deserues to beare,
Sharply Satirick was he, and that way
He went, since that his being, to this day
Few have attempted, and I surely thinke
Those wordes shall hardly be set downe with inke;
Shall scorch and blast, so as his could, where he,
Would inflict vengeance, and be it said of thee,
Shakespeare, thou hadst as smooth a Comicke vaine,
Fitting the socke, and in thy naturall braine,
As strong conception, and as Cleere a rage,
As any one that trafiqu'd with the stage.
Amongst these Samuel Daniel, whom if I
May spake of, but to sensure doe denie,
Onely have heard some wisemen him rehearse,
To be too much Historian in verse;
His rimes were smooth, his meeters well did close
But yet his maner better fitted prose:
Next these, learn'd Johnson, in this List I bring,
Who had drunke deepe of the Pierian spring,
Whose knowledge did him worthily prefer,
And long was Lord here of the Theater,
Who in opinion made our learn'st to sticke,
Whether in Poems rightly dramatique,
Strong Seneca or Plautus, he or they,
Should beare the Buskin, or the Socke away.
Others againe here liued in my dayes,
That have of us deserued no lesse praise
For their translations, then the daintiest wit
That on Parnassus thinks, he highst doth sit,
And for a chaire may mongst the Muses call,
As the most curious maker of them all;
As reverent Chapman, who hath brought to us,
Musæus, Homer and Hesiodus
Out of the Greeke; and by his skill hath reard
Them to that height, and to our tongue endear'd,
That were those Poets at this day aliue,
To see their bookes thus with us to suruiue,
They would think, hauing neglected them so long,
They had bin written in the English tongue.
And Siluester who from the French more weake,

Made Bartas of his sixe dayes labour speake
In naturall English, who, had he there stayd,
He had done well, and never had bewraid
His owne inuention, to have bin so poore
Who still wrote lesse, in striuing to write more.
Then dainty Sands that hath to English done,
Smooth sliding Ouid, and hath made him run
With so much sweetnesse and unusuall grace,
As though the neatnesse of the English pace,
Should tell the letting Lattine that it came
But slowly after, as though stiff and lame.
So Scotland sent us hither, for our owne
That man, whose name I ever would have knowne,
To stand by mine, that most ingenious knight,
My Alexander, to whom in his right,
I want extreamely, yet in speaking thus
I doe but shew the love, that was twixt us,
And not his numbers which were brave and hie,
So like his mind, was his clear Poesie,
And my deare Drummond to whom much I owe
For his much love, and proud I was to know,
His poesie, for which two worthy men,
I Menstry still shall love, and Hauthorne-den.
Then the two Beamounts and my Browne arose,
My deare companions whom I freely chose
My bosome friends; and in their severall wayes,
Rightly borne Poets, and in these last dayes,
Men of much note, and no lesse nobler parts,
Such as have freely tould to me their hearts,
As I have mine to them; but if you shall
Say in your knowledge, that these be not all
Have writ in numbers, be inform'd that I
Only my selfe, to these few men doe tye,
Whose works oft printed, set on every post,
To publique censure subiect have bin most;
For such whose poems, be they nere so rare,
In priuate chambers, that incloistered are,
And by transcription daintyly must goe;
As though the world unworthy were to know,
Their rich composures, let those men that keepe
These wonderous reliques in their judgement deepe;
And cry them up so, let such Peeces bee
Spoke of by those that shall come after me,
I passe not for them: nor doe meane to run,
In quest of these, that them applause have wonne,
Upon our Stages in these latter dayes,
That are so many, let them have their bayes
That doe deserue it; let those wits that haunt

Those publique circuits, let them freely chaunt
Their fine Composures, and their praise pursue
And so my deare friend, for this time adue.

Could there be words found to expresse my losse,
There were some hope, that this my heauy crosse
Might be sustained, and that wretched I
Might once finde comfort: but to have him die
Past all degrees that was so deare to me;
As but comparing him with others, hee
Was such a thing, as if some Power should say
I'le take Man on me, to shew men the way
What a friend should be. But words come so short
Of him, that when I thus would him report,
I am undone, and hauing nought to say,
Mad at my selfe, I throwe my penne away,
And beate my breast, that there should be a woe
So high, that words cannot attaine thereto.
T'is strange that I from my abundant breast,
Who others sorrowes have so well exprest:
Yet I by this in little time am growne
So poore, that I want to expresse mine owne.
I thinke the Fates perceiuing me to beare
My worldly crosses without wit or feare:
Nay, with what scorne I eVer have derided,
Those plagues that for me they have oft prouided,
Drew them to counsaile; nay, conspired rather,
And in this businesse laid their heads together
To finde some one plague, that might me subuert,
And at an instant breake my stubborne heart;
They did indeede, and onely to this end
They tooke from me this more then man, or friend.
Hard-hearted Fates, your worst thus have you done,
Then let us see what lastly you have wonne
By this your rigour, in a course so strict,
Why see, I beare all that you can inflict:
And hee from heaven your poore reuenge to view;
Laments my losse of him, but laughes at you,
Whilst I against you execrations breath;
Thus are you scorn'd aboue, and curst beneath.
Me thinks that man (unhappy though he be)
Is now thrice happy in respect of me,
Who hath no friend; for that in hauing none
He is not stirr'd as I am, to bemone
My miserable losse, who but in vaine,

May ever looke to find the like againe.
This more then mine own selfe; that who had seene
His care of me where ever I had beene,
And had not knowne his actiue spirit before,
Vpon some brave thing working evermore:
He would have sworne that to no other end
He had been borne: but onely for my friend.
I had been happy if nice Nature had
(Since now my lucke falls out to be so bad)
Made me unperfect, either of so soft
And yeelding temper, that lamenting oft,
I into teares my mournefull selfe might melt;
Or else so dull, my losse not to have felt.
I have by my too deare experience bought,
That fooles and mad men, whom I ever thought
The most unhappy, are in deede not so:
And therefore I lesse pittie can bestowe
(Since that my sence, my sorrowe so can sound)
On those in Bedlam that are bound,
And scarce feele scourging; and when as I meete
A foole by Children followed in the Streete,
Thinke I (poor wretch) thou from my griefe art free,
Nor couldst thou feele it, should it light on thee;
But that I am a Christian, and am taught
By him who with his precious bloud me bought,
Meekly like him my crosses to endure,
Else would they please me well, that for their cure,
When as they feele their conscience doth them brand,
Vpon themselues dare lay a violent hand;
Not suffering Fortune with her murdering knife,
Stand like a Surgeon working on the life,
Deserting this part, that joynt off to cut,
Shewing that Artire, ripping then that gut,
Whilst the dull beastly World with her squint eye,
Is to behold the strange Anatomie.
I am persuaded that those which we read
To be man-haters, were not so indeed,
The Athenian Timon, and beside him more
Of which the Latines, as the Greekes have store;
Nor not did they all humane manners hate,
Nor yet maligne mans dignity and state.
But finding our fraile life how every day,
It like a bubble vanisheth away:
For this condition did mankinde detest,
Farre more incertaine then that of the beast.
Sure heaven doth hate this world and deadly too,
Else as it hath done it would never doe,
For if it did not, it would ne're permit

A man of so much vertue, knowledge, wit,
Of naturall goodnesse, supernaturall grace,
Whose courses when considerately I trace
Into their ends, and diligently looke,
They serue me for Oeconomike booke.
By which this rough world I not onely stemme,
In goodnesse but grow learn'd by reading them.
O pardon me, it my much sorrow is,
Which makes me use this long Parenthesis;
Had heaven this world not hated as I say,
In height of life it had not, tane away
A spirit so brave, so actiue, and so free,
That such a one who would not wish to bee,
Rather then weare a Crowne, by Armes though got,
So fast a friend, so true a Patriot.
In things concerning both the worlds so wise,
Besides so liberall of his faculties,
That where he would his industrie bestowe,
He would have done, e're one could think to doe.
No more talke of the working of the Starres,
For plenty, scarcenesse, or for peace, or Warres:
They are impostures, therefore get you hence
With all your Planets, and their influence.
No more doe I care into them to looke,
Then in some idle Chiromantick booke,
Shewing the line of life, and Venus mount,
Nor yet no more would I of them account,
Then what that tells me, since what that so ere
Might promise man long life: of care and feare,
By nature freed, a conscience cleare, and quiet,
His health, his constitution, and his diet;
Counting a hundred, fourscore at the least,
Propt up by prayers, yet more to be encreast,
All these should faile, and in his fiftieth yeare
He should expire, henceforth let none be deare,
To me at all, lest for my haplesse sake,
Before their time heaven from the world them take,
And leave me wretched to lament their ends
As I doe his, who was a thousand friends.

UPON THE DEATH OF THE LAY OLIVE STANHOPE

Canst thou depart and be forgotten so,
STANHOPE thou canst not, no deare STANHOPE, no:
But in despight of death the world shall see,
That Muse which so much graced was by thee

Can black Obliuion vtterly out-braue,
And set thee up aboue thy silent Graue.
I meruail'd much the Derbian Nimphes were dumbe,
Or of those Muses, what should be become,
That of all those, the mountaines there among,
Not one this while thy Epicediumsung;
But so it is, when they of thee were reft,
They all those hills, and all those Riuers left,
And sullen growne, their former seates remoue,
Both from cleare Darwin, and from siluer Doue,
And for thy losse, they greeued are so sore,
That they have vow'd they will come there no more;
But leaue thy losse to me, that I should rue thee,
Unhappy man, and yet I never knew thee:
Me thou didst love unseene, so did I thee,
It was our spirits that lov'd then and not wee;
Therefore without profanenesse I may call
The love betwixt us, love spirituall:
But that which thou affectedst was so true,
As that thereby thee perfectly I knew;
And now that spirit, which thou so lov'dst, still mine,
Shall offer this a Sacrifice to thine,
And reare this Trophe, which for thee shall last,
When this most beastly Iron age is past;
I am perswaded, whilst we two have slept,
Our soules have met, and to each other wept,
That destenie so strongly should forbid,
Our bodies to conuerse as oft they did:
For certainly refined spirits doe know,
As doe the Angels, and doe here belowe
Take the fruition of that endlesse blisse,
As those aboue doe, and what each one is.
They see diuinely, and as those there doe,
They know each others wills, so soules can too.
About that dismall time, thy spirit hence flew,
Mine much was troubled, but why, I not knew,
In dull and sleepy sounds, it often left me,
As of it selfe it ment to have bereft me,
I asked it what the cause was, of such woe,
Or what it might be, that might vexe it so,
But it was deafe, nor my demand would here,
But when that ill newes came, to touch mine eare,
I straightwayes found this watchfull sperit of mine,
Troubled had bin to take it leaue of thine,
For when fate found, what nature late had done,
How much from heaven, she for the earth had won
By thy deare birth; said, that it could not be
In so yong yeares, what it perceiu'd in thee,

But nature sure, had fram'd thee long before;
And as Rich Misers of their mighty store,
Keepe the most precious longst, so from times past,
She onely had reserued thee till the last;
So did thy wisedome, not thy youth behold,
And tooke thee hence, in thinking thou wast old.
Thy shape and beauty often have to me
Bin highly praysed, which I thought might be,
Truely reported, for a spirit so brave,
Which heaven to thee so bountifully gave;
Nature could not in recompence againe,
In some rich lodging but to entertaine.
Let not the world report then, that the Peake,
Is but a rude place only vast and bleake;
And nothing hath to boast of but her Lead,
When she can say that happily she bred
Thee, and when she shall of her wonders tell
Wherein she doth all other Tracts excell,
Let her account thee greatst, and still to time
Of all the rest, accord thee for the prime.

TO MASTER WILIAM JEFFREYS, CHAPLAINE TO THE LORD AMBASSADOUR IN SPAINE

My noble friend, you challenge me to write
To you in verse, and often you recite,
My promise to you, and to send you newes;
As 'tis a thing I very seldome use,
And I must write of State, if to Madrid,
A thing our Proclamations here forbid,
And that word State such Latitude doth beare,
As it may make me very well to feare
To write, nay speake at all, these let you know
Your power on me, yet not that I will showe
The love I beare you, in that lofty height,
So cleere expression, or such words of weight,
As into Spanish if they were translated,
Might make the Poets of that Realme amated;
Yet these my least were, but that you extort
These numbers from me, when I should report
In home-spunne prose, in good plaine honest words
The newes our wofull England us affords.
The Muses here sit sad, and mute the while
A sort of swine unseasonably defile
Those sacred springs, which from the by-clift hill
Dropt their pure Nectar into every quill;
In this with State, I hope I doe not deale,

This onely tends the Muses common-weale.
What canst thou hope, or looke for from his pen,
Who lives with beasts, though in the shapes of men,
And what a poore few are we honest still,
And dare to be so, when all the world is ill.
I finde this age of our markt with this Fate,
That honest men are still precipitate
Under base villaines, which till th' earth can vent
This her last brood, and wholly hath them spent,
Shall be so, then in reuolution shall
Vertue againe arise by vices fall;
But that shall I not see, neither will I
Maintaine this, as one doth a Prophesie,
That our King Iames to Rome shall surely goe,
And from his chaire the Pope shall ouerthrow.
But O this world is so giuen up to hell,
That as the old Giants, which did once rebell,
Against the Gods, so this now-liuing race
Dare sin, yet stand, and leere heaven in the face.
But soft my Muse, and make a little stay,
Surely thou art not rightly in thy way,
To my good Ieffrayes was not I about
To write, and see, I suddainely am out,
This is pure Satire, that thou speak'st, and I
Was first in hand to write an Elegie.
To tell my countreys shame I not delight.
But doe bemoane 't I am no Democrite:
O God, though Vertue mightily doe grieue
For all this world, yet will I not beleeue
But that shees faire and lovely, and that she
So to the period of the world shall be;
Else had she beene forsaken (sure) of all,
For that so many sundry mischiefes fall
Vpon her dayly, and so many take
Armes up against her, as it well might make
Her to forsake her nature, and behind,
To leave no step for future time to find,
As she had never beene, for he that now
Can doe her most disgrace, him they alow
The times chiefe Champion, and he is the man,
The prize, and Palme that absolutely wanne,
For where Kings Clossets her free seat hath bin
She neere the Lodge, not suffered is to Inne,
For ignorance against her stands in state,
Like some great porter at a Pallace gate;
So dull and barbarous lately are we growne,
And there are some this slavery that have sowne,
That for mans knowledge it enough doth make,

If he can learne, to read an Almanacke;
By whom that trash of Amadis de Gaule,
Is held an author most authenticall,
And things we have like Noblemen that be
In little time, which I have hope to see
Vpon their foot-clothes, as the streets they ride
To have their hornebookes at their girdles ti'd.
But all their superfluity of spite
On vertues hand-maid Poesy doth light,
And to extirpe her all their plots they lay,
But to her ruine they shall misse the way,
For his alone the Monuments of wit,
Aboue the rage of Tyrants that doe sit,
And from their strength, not one himselfe can save,
But they shall tryumph o'r his hated grave.
In my conceipt, friend, thou didst never see
A righter Madman then thou hast of me,
For now as Elegiack I bewaile
These poor base times; then suddainely I raile
And am Satirick, not that I inforce
My selfe to be so, but euen as remorse,
Or hate, in the proud fulnesse of their hight
Master my fancy, just so doe I write.
But gentle friend as soone shall I behold
That stone of which so many have us tould,
(Yet never any to this day could make)
The great Elixar or to undertake
The Rose-crosse knowledge which is much like that
A Tarrying-iron for fooles to labour at,
As ever after I may hope to see,
(A plague upon this beastly world for me,)
Wit so respected as it was of yore;
And if hereafter any it restore,
It must be those that yet for many a yeare,
Shall be unborne that must inhabit here,
And such in vertue as shall be asham'd
Almost to heare their ignorant Grandsires nam'd,
With whom so many noble spirits then liu'd,
That were by them of all reward depriu'd.
My noble friend, I would I might have quit
This age of these, and that I might have writ,
Before all other, how much the brave pen,
Had here bin honoured of the English men;
Goodnesse and knowledge, held by them in prise,
How hatefull to them Ignorance and vice;
But it falls out the contrary is true,
And so my Ieffreyes for this time adue.

UPON THE DEATH OF MISTRIS ELIANOR FALLOWFIELD

Accursed Death, what neede was there at all
Of thee, or who to councell thee did call;
The subiect whereupon these lines I spend
For thee was most unfit, her timelesse end
Too soone thou wroughtst, too neere her thou didst stand;
Thou shouldst have lent thy leane and meager hand
To those who oft the help thereof beseech,
And can be cured by no other Leech.
In this wide world how many thousands be,
That hauing past fourescore, doe call for thee.
The wretched debtor in the Iayle that lies,
Yet cannot this his Creditor suffice
Doth woe thee oft with many a sigh and teare,
Yet thou art coy, and him thou wilt not heare.
The Captiue slave that tuggeth at the Oares,
And underneath the Bulls tough sinewes rores,
Begs at thy hand, in lieu of all his paines,
That thou wouldst but release him of his chaines;
Yet thou a niggard listenest not thereto,
With one short gaspe which thou mightst easily do,
But thou couldst come to her ere there was neede,
And euen at once destroy both flower and seede.
But cruell Death if thou so barbarous be,
To those so goodly, and so young as shee;
That in their teeming thou wilt shew thy spight;
Either from marriage thou wilt Maides affright,
Or in their wedlock, Widowes liues to chuse
Their Husbands bed, and vtterly refuse,
Fearing conception; so shalt thou thereby
Extirpate mankinde by thy cruelty.
If after direfull Tragedy thou thirst,
Extinguish Himens Torches at the first;
Build Funerall pyles, and the sad pavement strewe,
With mournfull Cypresse, and the pale-leau'd Yewe.
Away with Roses, Myrtle, and with Bayes;
Ensignes of mirth, and iollity, as these;
Never at Nuptials used be againe,
But from the Church the new Bride entertaine
With weeping Nenias, ever and among,
As at departings be sad Requiems song.
Lucina by th' olde Poets that wert sayd,
Women in Childe-birth evermore to ayde,
Because thine Altars, long have layne neglected:
Nor as they should, thy holy fiers reflected

Vpon thy Temples, therefore thou doest flye,
And wilt not helpe them in necessitie.
Thinking upon thee, I doe often muse,
Whether for thy deare sake I should accuse
Nature or Fortune, Fortune then I blame,
And doe impute it as her greatest shame,
To hast thy timelesse end, and soone agen
I vexe at Nature, nay I curse her then,
That at the time of need she was no stronger,
That we by her might have enjoy'd thee longer.
But whilst of these I with my selfe debate,
I call to minde how flinty-hearted Fate
Seaseth the olde, the young, the faire, the foule,
No thing on earth can Destinie controule:
But yet that Fate which hath of life bereft thee,
Still to eternall memory hath left thee,
Which thou enjoy'st by the deserued breath,
That many a great one hath not after death.

Michael Drayton – A Short Biography by Cyril Brett

Michael Drayton was born in 1563, at Hartshill, near Atherstone, in Warwickshire.

He became a page to Sir Henry Goodere, at Polesworth Hall: his own words give the best picture of his early years here. His education would seem to have been good, but ordinary; and it is very doubtful if he ever went to a university. Besides the authors mentioned in the Epistle to Henry Reynolds, he was certainly familiar with Ovid and Horace, and possibly with Catullus: while there seems no reason to doubt that he read Greek, though it is quite true that his references to Greek authors do not prove any first-hand acquaintance. He understood French, and read Rabelais and the French sonneteers, and he seems to have been acquainted with Italian. His knowledge of English literature was wide, and his judgement good: but his chief bent lay towards the history, legendary and otherwise, of his native country, and his vast stores of learning on this subject bore fruit in the Poly-Olbion.

While still at Polesworth, Drayton fell in love with his patron's younger daughter, Anne; and, though she married, in 1596, Sir Henry Raynsford of Clifford, Drayton continued his devotion to her for many years, and also became an intimate friend of her husband's, writing a sincere elegy on his death.

About February, 1591, Drayton paid a visit to London, and published his first work, the Harmony of the Church, a series of paraphrases from the Old Testament, in fourteen-syllabled verse of no particular vigour or grace. This book was immediately suppressed by order of Archbishop Whitgift, possibly because it was supposed to savour of Puritanism. The author, however, published another edition in 1610; indeed, he seems to have had a fondness for this style of work; for in 1604 he published a dull poem, Moyses in a Map of his Miracles, re-issued in 1630 as Moses his Birth and Miracles. Accompanying this piece, in 1630, were two other 'Divine poems': Noah's Floud, and David and Goliath. Noah's Floud is, in part, one of Drayton's happiest attempts at the catalogue style of bestiary; and Mr. Elton finds in it some foreshadowing of the manner of Paradise Lost. But, as a whole, Drayton's attempts in this direction deserve the oblivion into which they, in common with the similar productions of other authors, have fallen. In the dedication and preface to the Harmony of the Church are some of the few traces of Euphuism shown in Drayton's work; passages in the Heroical Epistles also occur to the mind He was always averse to affectation, literary or otherwise, and in Elegy VIII deliberately condemns Lyly's fantastic style.

Probably before Drayton went up to London, Sir Henry Goodere saw that he would stand in need of a patron more powerful than the master of Polesworth, and introduced him to the Earl and Countess of Bedford. Those who believe Drayton to have been a Pope in petty spite, identify the 'Idea' of his earlier poems with Lucy, Countess of Bedford; though they are forced to acknowledge as self-evident that the 'Idea' of his later work is Anne, Lady Raynsford. They then proceed to say that Drayton, after consistently honouring the Countess in his verse for twelve years, abruptly transferred his allegiance, not forgetting to heap foul abuse on his former patroness, out of pique at some temporary withdrawal of favour. Not only is this directly contrary to all we know and can infer of Drayton's character, but Mr. Elton has decisively disproved it by a summary of bibliographical and other evidence. Into the question it is here unnecessary to enter, and it has been mentioned only because it alone, of the many Drayton-controversies, has cast any slur on the poet's reputation.

In 1593, Drayton published Idea, the Shepherds Garland, in nine Eclogues; in 1606 he added a tenth, the best of all, to the new edition, and rearranged the order, so that the new eclogue became the ninth. In these Pastorals, while following the Shepherds Calendar in many ways, he already displays something of the sturdy independence which characterized him through life. He abandons Spenser's quasi-rustic dialect, and, while keeping to most of the pastoral conventions, such as the singing-match and threnody, he contrives to introduce something of a more natural and homely strain. He keeps the political allusions, notably in the Eclogue containing the song in praise of Beta, who is, of course, Queen Elizabeth. But an over-bold remark in the last line of that song was struck out in 1606; and the new eclogue has no political reference. He is not ashamed to allude directly to Spenser; and indeed his direct debts are limited to a few scattered phrases, as in the Ballad of Dowsabel. Almost to the end of his literary career, Drayton mentions Spenser with reverence and praise.

It is in the songs interspersed in the Eclogues that Drayton's best work at this time is to be found: already his metrical versatility is discernible; for though he doubtless remembered the many varieties of metre employed by Spenser in the Calendar, his verses already bear a stamp of their own. The long but impetuous lines, such as 'Trim up her golden tresses with Apollo's sacred tree', afford a striking contrast to the archaic romance-metre, derived from Sir Thopas and its fellows, which appears in Dowsabel, and it again to the melancholy, murmuring cadences of the lament for Elphin. It must, however, be confessed that certain of the songs in the 1593 edition were full of recondite conceits and laboured antitheses, and were rightly struck out, to be replaced by lovelier poems, in the edition of 1606. The song to Beta was printed in Englands Helicon, 1600; here, for the first time, appeared the song of Dead Love, and for the only time, Rowlands Madrigal. In these songs, Drayton offends least in grammar, always a weak point with him; in the body of the Eclogues, in the earlier Sonnets, in the Odes, occur the most extraordinary and perplexing inversions. Quite the most striking feature of the Eclogues, especially in their later form, is their bold attempt at greater realism, at a breaking-away from the conventional images and scenery.

Having paid his tribute to one poetic fashion, Drayton in 1594 fell in with the prevailing craze for sonneteering, and published Ideas Mirrour, a series of fifty-one 'amours' or sonnets, with two prefatory poems, one by Drayton and one by an unknown, signing himself Gorbo il fidele. The title of these poems

Drayton possibly borrowed from the French sonneteer, de Pontoux: in their style much recollection of Sidney, Constable, and Daniel is traceable. They are ostensibly addressed to his mistress, and some of them are genuine in feeling; but many are merely imitative exercises in conceit; some, apparently, trials in metre. These amours were again printed, with the title of 'sonnets', in 1599, 1600, 1602, 1603, 1605, 1608, 1610, 1613, 1619, and 1631, during the poet's lifetime. It is needless here to discuss whether Drayton were the 'rival poet' to Shakespeare, whether these sonnets were really addressed to a man, or merely to the ideal Platonic beauty; for those who are interested in these points, I subjoin references to the sonnets which touch upon them. From the prentice-work evident in many of the Amours, it would seem that certain of them are among Drayton's earliest poems; but others show a craftsman not meanly advanced in his art. Nevertheless, with few exceptions, this first 'bundle of sonnets' consists rather of trials of skill, bubbles of the mind; most of his sonnets which strike the reader as touched or penetrated with genuine passion belong to the editions from 1599 onwards; implying that his love for Anne Goodere, if at all represented in these poems, grew with his years, for the 'love-parting' is first found in the edition of 1619. But for us the question should not be, are these sonnets genuine representations of the personal feeling of the poet? but rather, how far do they arouse or echo in us as individuals the universal passion? There are at least some of Drayton's sonnets which possess a direct, instant, and universal appeal, by reason of their simple force and straightforward ring; and not in virtue of any subtle charm of sound and rhythm, or overmastering splendour of diction or thought. Ornament vanishes, and soberness and simplicity increase, as we proceed in the editions of the sonnets. Drayton's chief attempt in the jewelled or ornamental style appeared in 1595, with the title of Endimion and Phoebe, and was, in a sense, an imitation of Marlowe's Hero and Leander. Hero and Leander is, as Swinburne says, a shrine of Parian marble, illumined from within by a clear flame of passion; while Endimion and Phoebe is rather a curiously wrought tapestry, such as that in Mortimer's Tower, woven in splendid and harmonious colours, wherein, however, the figures attain no clearness or subtlety of outline, and move in semi-conventional scenery. It is, none the less, graceful and impressive, and of a like musical fluency with other poems of its class, such as Venus and Adonis, or Salmacis and Hermaphrodius. Parts of it were re-set and spoilt in a 1606 publication of Drayton's, called The Man in the Moone.

In 1593 and 1594 Drayton also published his earliest pieces on the mediaeval theme of the 'Falls of the Illustrious'; they were Peirs Gavesson and Matilda the faire and chaste daughter of the Lord Robert Fitzwater. Here Drayton followed in the track of Boccaccio, Lydgate, and the Mirrour for Magistrates, walking in the way which Chaucer had derided in his Monkes Tale: and with only too great fidelity does Drayton adapt himself to the dullnesses of his model: fine rhetoric is not altogether wanting, and there is, of course, the consciousness that these subjects deal with the history of his beloved country, but neither these, nor Robert, Duke of Normandy (1596), nor Great Cromwell, Earl of Essex (1607 and 1609), nor the Miseries of Margaret (1627) can escape the charge of tediousness. England's Heroical Epistles were first published in 1597, and other editions, of 1598, 1599, and 1602, contain new epistles. These are Drayton's first attempt to strike out a new and original vein of English poetry: they are a series of letters, modelled on Ovid's Heroides, addressed by various pairs of lovers, famous in English history, to each other, and arranged in chronological order, from Henry II and Rosamond to Lady Jane Grey and Lord Guilford Dudley. They are, in a sense, the most important of Drayton's writings, and they have certainly been the most popular, up to the early nineteenth century. In these poems Drayton foreshadowed, and probably inspired, the smooth style of Fairfax, Waller, and Dryden. The metre, the grammar, and the thought, are all perfectly easy to follow, even though he employs many of the Ovidian 'turns' and 'clenches'. A certain attempt at realization of the different characters is observable, but the poems are fine rhetorical exercises rather than realizations of the dramatic and passionate possibilities of their themes. In 1596, Drayton, as we have seen, published the Mortimeriados, a kind of epic, with Mortimer as its hero, of the wars between King Edward II and the Barons. It was written in the seven-line stanza of Chaucer's Troilus and Cressida and Spenser's Hymns. On its republication in 1603, with the title of the Barons' Wars, the metre was changed to ottava rima, and Drayton showed, in an excellent preface, that he fully appreciated the principles and the subtleties of the metrical art. While possessing many fine passages, the Barons' Wars is somewhat dull, lacking much of the poetry of the older version; and does not escape from Drayton's own criticism of Daniel's Chronicle Poems: 'too much historian in verse, ... His rhymes were smooth, his metres well did close, But yet his manner better fitted prose'. The description of Mortimer's Tower in the sixth book recalls the ornate style of Endimion and Phoebe, while the fifth book, describing the miseries of King Edward, is the most moving and dramatic. But there is a general lifelessness and lack of movement for which these purple passages barely atone. The cause of the production of so many chronicle poems about this time has been supposed to be the desire of showing the horrors of civil war, at a time when the queen was growing old, and no successor had, as it seemed, been accepted. Also they were a kind of parallel to the Chronicle Play; and Drayton, in any case even if we grant him to have been influenced by the example of Daniel, never needed much incentive to treat a national theme.

About this time, we find Drayton writing for the stage. It seems unnecessary here to discuss whether the writing of plays is evidence of Drayton's poverty, or his versatility; but the fact remains that he had a hand in the production of about twenty. Of these, the only one which certainly survives is The first part of the true and honorable historie, of the life of Sir John Oldcastle, the good Lord Cobham, &c. It is practically impossible to distinguish Drayton's share in this curious play, and it does not, therefore, materially assist the elucidation of the question whether he had any dramatic feeling or skill. It can be safely affirmed that the dramatic instinct was nor uppermost in his mind; he was a Seneca rather than a Euripides: but to deny him all dramatic idea, as does Dr. Whitaker, is too severe. There is decided, if slender, dramatic skill and feeling in certain of the Nymphals. Drayton's persons are usually, it must be said, rather figures in a tableau, or series of tableaux; but in the second and seventh Nymphals, and occasionally in the tenth, there is real dramatic movement. Closely connected with this question is the consideration of humour, which is wrongly denied to Drayton. Humour is observable first, perhaps, in the Owle (1604); then in the Ode to his Rival (1619); and later in the Nymphidia, Shepheards Sirena, and Muses Elyzium. The second Nymphal shows us the quiet laughter, the humorous twinkle, with which Drayton writes at times. The subject is an [Greek: agôn] or contest between two shepherds for the affections of a nymph called Lirope: Lalus is a vale-bred swain, of refined and elegant manners, skilled, nevertheless, in all manly sports and exercises; Cleon, no less a master in physical prowess, was nurtured by a hind in the mountains; the contrast between their manners is admirably sustained: Cleon is rough, inclined to be rude and scoffing, totally without tact, even where his mistress is concerned. Lalus remembers her upbringing and her tastes; he makes no unnecessary or ostentatious display of wealth; his gifts are simple and charming, while Cleon's are so grotesquely unsuited to a swain, that it is tempting to suppose that Drayton was quietly satirizing Marlowe's Passionate Shepherd. Lirope listens gravely to the swains in turn, and makes demure but provoking answers, raising each to the height of hope, and then casting them both down into the depths of despair; finally she refuses both, yet without altogether killing hope. Her first answer is a good specimen of her banter and of Drayton's humour.

On the accession of James I, Drayton hastened to greet the King with a somewhat laboured song To the Maiestie of King James; but this poem was apparently considered to be premature: he cried Vivat Rex, without having said, Mortua est eheu Regina, and accordingly he suffered the penalty of his 'forward pen', and was severely neglected by King and Court. Throughout James's reign a darker and more satirical mood possesses Drayton, intruding at times even into his strenuous recreation-ground, the Poly-Olbion, and manifesting itself more directly in his satires, the Owle (1604), the Moon-Calfe (1627), the Man in the Moone (1606), and his verse-letters and elegies; while his disappointment with the times, the country, and the King, flashes out occasionally even in the Odes, and is heard in his last publication, the Muses Elizium (1630). To counterbalance the disappointment in his hopes from the King, Drayton found a new and life-long friend in Walter Aston, of Tixall, in Staffordshire; this gentleman was created Knight of the Bath by James, and made Drayton one of his esquires. By Aston's 'continual bounty' the poet was able to devote himself almost entirely to more congenial literary work; for, while Meres speaks of the Poly-Olbion in 1598, and we may easily see that Drayton had the idea of that work at least as early as 1594, yet he cannot have been able to give much time to it till now. Nevertheless, the 'declining and corrupt times' worked on Drayton's mind and grieved and darkened his soul, for we must remember that he was perfectly prosperous then and was not therefore incited to satire by bodily want or distress.

In 1604 he published the Owle, a mild satire, under the form of a moral fable of government, reminding the reader a little of the Parlement of Foules. The Man in the Moone (1606) is partly a recension of Endimion and Phoebe, but is a heterogeneous mass of weakly satire, of no particular merit. The Moon-Calfe (1627) is Drayton's most savage and misanthropic excursion into the region of Satire; in which, though occasionally nobly ironic, he is more usually coarse and blustering, in the style of Marston. In 1605 Drayton brought out his first 'collected poems', from which the Eclogues and the Owle are omitted; and in 1606 he published his Poemes Lyrick and Pastorall, Odes, Eglogs, The Man in the Moone. Of these the Eglogs are a recension of the Shepherd's Garland of 1593: we have already spoken of The Man in the Moone. The Odes are by far the most important and striking feature of the book. In the preface, Drayton professes to be following Pindar, Anacreon, and Horace, though, as he modestly implies, at a great distance. Under the title of Odes he includes a variety of subjects, and a variety of metres; ranging from an Ode to his Harp or to his Criticks, to a Ballad of Agincourt, or a poem on the Rose compared with his Mistress. In the edition of 1619 appeared several more Odes, including some of the best; while many of the others underwent careful revision, notably the Ballad. 'Sing wee the Rose,' perhaps because of its unintelligibility, and the Ode to his friend John Savage, perhaps because too closely imitated from Horace, were omitted. Drayton was not the first to use the term Ode for a lyrical poem, in English: Soothern in 1584, and Daniel in 1592 had preceded him; but he was the first to give the name popularity in England, and to lift the kind as Ronsard had lifted it in France; and till the time of Cowper no other English poet showed mastery of the short, staccato measure of the Anacreontic as distinct from the Pindaric Ode. In the Odes Drayton shows to the fullest extent his metrical versatility: he touches the Skeltonic metre, the long ten-syllabled line of the Sacrifice to Apollo; and ascends from the smooth and melodious rhythms of the New Year through the inspiring harp-tones of the Virginian Voyage to the clangour and swing of the Ballad of Agincourt. His grammar is possibly more distorted here than anywhere, but, as Mr. Elton says, 'these are the obstacles of any poet who uses measures of four or six syllables.' His tone throughout is rather that of the harp, as played, perhaps, in Polesworth Hall, than that of any other instrument; but in 1619 Drayton has taken to him the lute of Carew and his compeers. In 1619 the style is lighter, the fancy gayer, more exquisite, more recondite. Most of his few metaphysical conceits are to be found in these later Odes, as in the Heart, the Valentine, and the Crier. In the comparison of the two editions the nobler, if more strained, tone of the earlier is obvious; it is still Elizabethan, in its nobility of ideal and purpose, in its enthusiasm, in its belief and confidence in England and her men; and this even though we catch a glimpse of the Jacobean woe in the Ode to John Savage: the 1619 Odes are of a different world; their spirit is lighter, more insouciant in appearance, though perhaps studiedly so; the rhythms are more fantastic, with less of strength and firmness, though with more of grace and superficial beauty; even the very textual alterations, while usually increasing the grace and the music of the lines, remind the reader that something of the old spontaneity and freshness is gone.

In 1607 and 1609, Drayton published two editions of the last and weakest of his mediaeval poems—the Legend of Great Cromwell; and for the next few years he produced nothing new, only attending to the publication of certain reprints and new editions. During this time, however, he was working steadily at the Poly-Olbion, helped by the patronage of Aston and of Prince Henry. In 1612-13, Drayton burst upon an indifferent world with the first part of the great poem, containing eighteen songs; the title-page will give the best idea of the contents and plan of the book: 'Poly-Olbion or a Chorographicall Description of the Tracts, Riuers, Mountaines, Forests, and other Parts of this renowned Isle of Great Britaine, With intermixture of the most Remarquable Stories, Antiquities, Wonders, Rarityes, Pleasures, and Commodities of the same: Digested in a Poem by Michael Drayton, Esq. With a Table added, for direction to those occurrences of Story and Antiquities, whereunto the Course of the Volume easily leades not.' &c. On this work Drayton had been engaged for nearly the whole of his poetical career. The learning and research displayed in the poem are extraordinary, almost equalling the erudition of Selden in his Annotations to each Song. The first part was, for various reasons, a drug in the market, and Drayton found great difficulty in securing a publisher for the second part. But during the years from 1613 to 1622, he became acquainted with Drummond of Hawthornden through a common friend, Sir William Alexander of Menstry, afterwards Earl of Stirling. In 1618, Drayton starts a correspondence; and towards the end of the year mentions that he is corresponding also with Andro Hart, bookseller, of Edinburgh. The subject of his letter was probably the publication of the Second Part; which Drayton alludes to in a letter of 1619 thus: 'I have done twelve books more, that is from the eighteenth book, which was Kent, if you note it; all the East part and North to the river Tweed; but it lies by me; for the booksellers and I are in terms; they are a company of base knaves, whom I both scorn and kick at.' Finally, in 1622, Drayton got Marriott, Grismand, and Dewe, of London, to take the work, and it was published with a dedication to Prince Charles, who, after his brother's death, had given Drayton patronage. Drayton's preface to the Second Part is well worth quoting:

'To any that will read it. When I first undertook this Poem, or, as some very skilful in this kind have pleased to term it, this Herculean labour, I was by some virtuous friends persuaded, that I should receive much comfort and encouragement therein; and for these reasons; First, that it was a new, clear, way, never before gone by any; then, that it contained all the Delicacies, Delights, and Rarities of this renowned Isle, interwoven with the Histories of the Britons, Saxons, Normans, and the later English: And further that there is scarcely any of the Nobility or Gentry of this land, but that he is in some way or other by his Blood interested therein. But it hath fallen out otherwise; for instead of that comfort, which my noble friends (from the freedom of their spirits) proposed as my due, I have met with barbarous ignorance, and base detraction; such a cloud hath the Devil drawn over the world's judgment, whose opinion is in few years fallen so far below all ballatry, that the lethargy is incurable: nay, some of the Stationers, that had the selling of the First Part of this Poem, because it went not so fast away in the sale, as some of their beastly and abominable trash, (a shame both to our language and nation) have either despitefully left out, or at least carelessly neglected the Epistles to the Readers, and so have cozened the buyers with unperfected books; which these that have undertaken the Second Part, have been forced to amend in the First, for the small number that are yet remaining in their hands. And some of our outlandish, unnatural, English, (I know not how otherwise to express them) stick not to say that there is nothing in this Island worth studying for, and take a great pride to be ignorant in any thing thereof; for these, since they delight in their folly, I wish it may be hereditary from them to their posterity, that their children may be begg'd for fools to the fifth generation, until it may be beyond the memory of man to know that there was ever other of their families: neither can this deter me from going on with Scotland, if means and time do not hinder me, to perform as much as I have promised in my First Song:

Till through the sleepy main, to Thuly I have gone,
And seen the Frozen Isles, the cold Deucalidon,
Amongst whose iron Rocks, grim Saturn yet remains
Bound in those gloomy caves with adamantine chains.

And as for those cattle whereof I spake before, Odi profanum vulgus, et arceo, of which I account them, be they never so great, and so I leave them. To my friends, and the lovers of my labours, I wish all happiness.
Michael Drayton.'

The Poly-Olbion as a whole is easy and pleasant to read; and though in some parts it savours too much of a mere catalogue, yet it has many things truly poetical. The best books are perhaps the XIII, XIV and XV, where he is on his own ground, and therefore naturally at his best. It is interesting to notice how much attention and space he devotes to Wales. He describes not only the 'wonders' but also the fauna and flora of each district; and of the two it would seem that the flowers interested him more. Though he was a keen observer of country sights and sounds (a fact sufficiently attested by the Nymphidia and the Nymphals), it is evident that his interest in most things except flowers was rather momentary or conventional than continuous and heart-felt; but of the flowers he loves to talk, whether he weaves us a garland for the Thame's wedding, or gives us the contents of a maund of simples; and his love, if somewhat homely and unimaginative, is apparent enough. But the main inspiration, as it is the main theme, of the Poly-Olbion is the glory and might and wealth, past, present, and future, of England, her possessions and her folk. Through all this glory, however, we catch the tone of Elizabethan sorrow over the 'Ruines of Time'; grief that all these mighty men and their works will perish and be forgotten, unless the poet makes them live for ever on the lips of men. Drayton's own voluminousness has defeated his purpose, and sunk his poem by its own bulk. Though it is difficult to go so far as Mr. Bullen, and say that the only thing better than a stroll in the Poly-Olbion is one in a Sussex lane, it is still harder to agree with Canon Beeching, that 'there are few beauties on the road', the beauties are many, though of a quietly rural type, and the road, if long and winding, is of good surface, while its cranks constitute much of its charm. It is doubtless, from the outside, an appalling poem in these days of epitomes and monographs, but it certainly deserves to be rescued from oblivion and read.

In 1618 Drayton contributed two Elegies to Henry FitzGeoffrey's Satyrs and Epigrames. These were on the Lady Penelope Clifton, and on 'the death of the three sonnes of the Lord Sheffield, drowned neere where Trent falleth into Humber'. Neither is remarkable save for far-fetched conceits; they were reprinted in 1610, and again, with many others, in the volume of 1627. In 1619 Drayton issued a folio collected edition of his works, and reprinted it in 1620. In 1627 followed a folio of wholly fresh matter, including the Battaile of Agincourt; the Miseries of Queene Margarite, Nimphidia, Quest of Cinthia, Shepheards Sirena, Moone-Calfe, and Elegies upon sundry occasions. The Battaile of Agincourt is a somewhat otiose expansion, with purple patches, of the Ballad; it is, nevertheless, Drayton's best lengthy piece on a historical theme. Of the Miseries of Queene Margarite and of the Moone-Calfe we have already spoken. The most notable piece in the book is the Nimphidia. This poem of the Court of Fairy has 'invention, grace, and humour', as Canon Beeching has said. It would be interesting to know exactly when it was composed and committed to paper, for it is thought that the three fairy poems in Herrick's Hesperides were written about 1626. In any case, Drayton's poem touches very little, and chiefly in the beginning, on the subject of any one of Herrick's three pieces. The style, execution, and impression left on the reader are quite different; even as they are totally unlike those of the Midsummer Night's Dream. Herrick's pieces are extraordinary combinations of the idea of 'King of Shadows', with a reality fantastically sober: the poems are steeped in moonlight. In Drayton all is clear day, or the most unromantic of nights; though everything is charming, there is no attempt at idealization, little of the higher faculty of imagination; but great realism, and much play of fancy. Herrick's verses were written by Cobweb and Moth together, Drayton's by Puck. Granting, however, the initial deficiency in subtlety of charm, the whole poem is inimitably graceful and piquant. The gay humour, the demure horror of the witchcraft, the terrible seriousness of the battle, wonderfully realize the mock-heroic gigantesque; and while there is not the minute accuracy of Gulliver in Lilliput, Drayton did not write for a sceptical or too-prying audience; quite half his readers believed more or less in fairies. In the metre of the poem Drayton again echoes that of the older romances, as he did in Dowsabel. In the Quest of Cinthia, while ostensibly we come to the real world of mortals, we are really in a non-existent land of pastoral convention, in the most pseudo-Arcadian atmosphere in which Drayton ever worked. The metre and the language are, however, charmingly managed. The Shepheards Sirena is a poem, apparently, 'where more is meant than meets the ear,' as so often in pastoral poetry; it is difficult to see exactly what is meant; but the Jacobean strain of doubt and fear is there, and the poem would seem to have been written some time earlier than 1627. The Elegies comprise a great variety of styles and themes; some are really threnodies, some verse-letters, some laments over the evil times, and one a summary of Drayton's literary opinions. He employs the couplet in his Elegies with a masterly hand, often with a deliberately rugged effect, as in his broader Marstonic satire addressed to William Browne; while the line of greater smoothness but equal strength is to be seen in the letters to Sandys and Jeffreys. He is fantastic and conceited in most of the threnodies; but, as is natural, that on his old friend, Sir Henry Raynsford, is least artificial and fullest of true feeling. The epistle to Henery Reynolds. Of Poets and Poesie shows Drayton as a sane and sagacious critic, ready to see the good, but keen to discern the weakness also; perhaps the clearest evidence of his critical skill is the way in which nearly all of his judgements on his contemporaries coincide with the received modern opinions.

In his later years Drayton enjoyed the patronage of the third Earl and Countess of Dorset; and in 1630 he published his last volume, the Muses Elizium, of which he dedicated the pastoral part to the Earl, and the three divine poems at the end to the Countess. The Muses Elizium proper consists of Ten Pastorals or Nymphals, prefaced by a Description of Elizium. The three divine poems have been mentioned before, and were Noah's Floud, Moses his Birth and Miracles, and David and Goliah. The Nymphals are the crown and summary of much of the best in Drayton's work. Here he departed from the conventional type of pastoral, even more than in the Shepherd's Garland; but to say that he sang of English rustic life would hardly be true: the sixth Nymphal, allowing for a few pardonable exaggerations by the competitors, is almost all English, if we except the names; so is the tenth with the same exception; the first and fourth might take place anywhere, but are not likely in any country; the second is more conventional; the fifth is almost, but not quite, English; the third, seventh, and ninth are avowedly classical in theme; while the eighth is a more delicate and subtle fairy poem than the Nymphidia. The fourth and tenth Nymphals are also touched with the sadder, almost satiric vein; the former inveighing against the English imitation of foreigners and love of extravagance in dress; while the tenth complains of the improvident and wasteful felling of trees in the English forests. This last Nymphal, though designedly an epilogue, is probably rather a warning than a despairing lament, even though we conceive the old satyr to be Drayton himself. As a whole the Nymphals show Drayton at his happiest and lightest in style and metre; at his moments of greatest serenity and even gaiety; an atmosphere of sunshine seems to envelope them all, though the sun sink behind a cloud in the last. His music now is that of a rippling stream, whereas in his earlier days he spoke weightier and more sonorous words, with a mouth of gold.

To estimate the poetical faculty of Drayton is a somewhat perplexing task; for, while rarely subtle, or rising to empyrean heights, he wrote in such varied styles, on such various themes, that the task, at first, seems that of criticizing many poets, not one. But through all his work runs the same eminently English spirit, the same honesty and clearness of idea, the same stolidity of purpose, and not infrequently of execution also; the same enthusiasm characterizes all his earlier, and much of his later work; the enthusiasm especially characteristic of Elizabethan England, and shown by Drayton in his passion for England and the English, in his triumphant joy in their splendid past, and his certainty of their future glory. As a poet, he lacked imagination and fine fury; he supplied their place by the airiest and clearest of fancies, by the strenuous labour of a great brain illumined by the steady flame of love for his country and for his lady. Mr. Courthope has said that he lacked loftiness and resolution of artistic purpose; without these, we ask, how could a man, not lavishly dowered with poetry in his soul, have achieved so much of it? It was his very fixity and loftiness of purpose, his English stubbornness and doggedness of resolution that enabled him to surmount so many obstacles of style and metre, of subject and thought. His two purposes, of glorifying his mistress and his friends, and of sounding England's glories past and future, while insisting on the dangers of a present decadence, never flagged or failed. All his poetry up to 1627 has this object directly or secondarily; and much after this date. Of the more abstract and universal aspects of his art he had not much conception; but he caught eagerly at the fashionable belief in the eternizing power of poetry; and had it not been that, where his patriotism was uppermost, he was deficient in humour and sense of proportion, he would have succeeded better: as it is, his more directly patriotic pieces are usually the dullest or longest of his works. He requires, like all other poets, the impulse of an absolutely personal and individual feeling, a moment of more intimate sympathy, to rouse him to his heights of song. Thus the Ballad of Agincourt is on the very theme of all patriotic themes that most attracted him; Virginian and other Voyages lay very close to his heart; and in certain sonnets to his lady lies his only imperishable work. Of sheer melody and power of song he had little, apart from his themes: he could not have sat down and written a few lark's or nightingale's notes about nothing as some of his contemporaries were able to do: he required the stimulus of a subject, and if he were really moved thereby he beat the music out. Only in one or two of the later Odes, and in the volumes of 1627 and 1630, does his music ever seem to flow from him naturally. Akin to this quality of broad and extensive workmanship, to this faculty of taking a subject and when writing, with all thought concentrated on it, rather than on the method of writing about it, is his strange lack of what are usually called 'quotations'. For this is not only due to the fact that he is little known; there are, besides, so few detached remarks or aphorisms that are separately quotable; so few examples of that curiosa felicitas of diction: lines like these,

Thy Bowe, halfe broke, is peec'd with old desire;
Her Bowe is beauty with ten thousand strings....

are rare enough. Drayton, in fact, comes as near controverting the statement Poeta nascitur, non fit, as any one in English literature: by diligent toil and earnest desire he won a place for himself in the second rank of English poets: through love he once set foot in the circle of the mightiest. Sincere he was always, simple often, sensuous rarely. His great industry, his careful study, and his great receptivity are shown in the unusual spectacle of a man who has sung well in the language of his youth, suddenly learning, in his age, the tongue spoken by the younger generation, and reproducing it with individuality and sureness of touch. It is in rhetoric, splendid or rugged, in argument, in plain statement or description, in the outline sketch of a picture, that Drayton excels; magic of atmosphere and colouring are rarely present. Stolidity is, perhaps, his besetting sin; yet it is the sign of a slow, not a dull, intellect; an intellect, like his heart, which never let slip what it had once taken to itself.

As a man Drayton would seem to have been an excellent type of the sturdy, clear-headed, but yet romantic and enthusiastic Englishman; gifted with much natural ability, sedulously increased by study;

quietly humorous, self-restrained; and if temporarily soured by disappointment and the disjointed times, yet emerging at last into a greater serenity, a more unadulterated gaiety than had ever before characterized him. It is possible, but from his clear and sane balance of mind improbable, that many of his light later poems are due to deliberate self-blinding and self-deception, a walking in enchanted lands of the mind.

Of Drayton's three known portraits the earliest shows him at the age of thirty-six, and is now in the National Portrait Gallery. A look of quiet, speculative melancholy seems to pervade it; there is, as yet, no moroseness, no evidence of severe conflict with the world, no shadow of stress or of doubt. The second and best-known portrait shows us Drayton at the age of fifty, and was engraved by Hole, as a frontispiece to the poems of 1619. Here a notable change has come over the face; the mouth is hardened, and depressed at the corners through disappointment and disillusionment; the eyes are full of a pathos increased by the puzzled and perturbed uplift of the brows. Yet a stubbornness and tenacity of purpose invests the features and reminds us that Drayton is of the old and sound Elizabethan stock, 'on evil days though fallen.' Let it be remembered, that he was in 1613, when the portrait was taken, in more or less prosperous circumstances; it was the sad degeneracy, the meanness and feebleness of the generation around him, that chiefly depressed and embittered him. The final portrait, now in the Dulwich Gallery, represents the poet as a man of sixty-five; and is quite in keeping with the sunnier and calmer tone of his later poetry. It is the face of one who has not emerged unscathed from the world's conflict, but has attained to a certain calm, a measure of tranquillity, a portion of content, who has learnt the lesson that there is a soul of goodness in things evil. The Hole portrait shows him with long hair, small 'goatee' beard, and aquiline nose drawn up at the nostrils: while the National portrait shows a type of nose and beard intermediate between the Hole and the Dulwich pictures: the general contour of the face, though the forehead is broad enough, is long and oval. Drayton seems to have been tall and thin, and to have been very susceptible of cold, and therefore to have hated Winter and the North. He is said to have shared in the supper which caused Shakespeare's death; but his own verses breathe the spirit of Milton's sonnet to Cyriack Skinner, rather than that of a devotee of Bacchus.

He died in 1631, probably December 23, and was buried under the North wall of Westminster Abbey. Meres's opinion of his character during his early life is as follows: 'As Aulus Persius Flaccus is reported among al writers to be of an honest life and vpright conuersation: so Michael Drayton, quem totics honoris et amoris causa nomino, among schollers, souldiours, Poets, and all sorts of people is helde for a man of uertuous disposition, honest conversation, and well gouerned cariage; which is almost miraculous among good wits in these declining and corrupt times, when there is nothing but rogery in villanous man, and when cheating and craftines is counted the cleanest wit, and soundest wisedome.' Fuller also, in a similar strain, says, 'He was a pious poet, his conscience having the command of his fancy, very temperate in his life, slow of speech, and inoffensive in company.'

A Chronology of Michael Drayton's Life and Works

1563   Drayton born at Hartshill, Warwickshire.
c. 1572   Drayton a page in the house of Sir Henry Goodere, at Polesworth.
c. 1574   Anne Goodere born
February, 1591 Drayton in London. Harmony of Church.
1593   Idea, the Shepherd's Garland. Legend of Peirs Gaveston.
1594   Ideas Mirrour. Matilda. Lucy Harrington becomes Countess of Bedford.

1595	Sir Henry Goodere the elder dies. Endimion and Phoebe, dedicated to Lucy Bedford.
1595-6	Anne Goodere married to Sir Henry Raynsford.
1596	Mortimeriados. Legends of Robert, Matilda, and Gaveston.
1597	England's Heroical Epistles.
1598	Drayton already at work on the Poly-Olbion.
1599	Epistles and Idea sonnets, new edition. (Date of Drayton portrait in National Portrait Gallery.)
1600	Sir John Oldcastle.
1602	New edition of Epistles and Idea.
1603	Drayton made an Esquire of the Bath, to Sir Walter Aston. To the Maiestie of King James. Barons' Wars.
1604	The Owle. A Pean Triumphall. Moyses in a Map of his Miracles.
1605	First collected edition of Poems. Another edition of Idea and Epistles.
1606	Poemes Lyrick and Pastorall. Odes. Eglogs. The Man in the Moone.
1607	Legend of Great Cromwell.
1608	Reprint of Collected Poems.
1609	Another edition of Cromwell.
1610	Reprint of Collected Poems.
1613	Reprint of Collected Poems. First Part of Poly-Olbion.
1618	Two Elegies in FitzGeoffrey's Satyrs and Epigrames.
1619	Collected Folio edition of Poems.
1620	Second edition of Elegies, and reprint of 1619 Poems.
1622	Poly-Olbion complete.
1627	Battle of Agincourt, Nymphidia, &c.
1630	Muses Elizium. Noah's Floud. Moses his Birth and Miracles. David and Goliah.
1631	Second edition of 1627 folio. Drayton dies December 23rd.
1636	Posthumous poem appeared in Annalia Dubrensia.
1637	Poems.

Michael Drayton – A Concise Bibliography

The Major Works

The Harmony of the Church (1591)
Idea, The Shepherd's Garland (1593)
Idea's Mirror (1594)
Peirs Gaveston (1593 or 1594)
Matilda (1594)
Endimion and Phoebe: Idea's Latmus (1595)
The Tragical Legend of Robert, Duke of Normandy (1596)
Mortimeriados (1596)
England's Heroicall Epistles (1597)
The First Part of the Life of Sir John Oldcastle (1600)
The Barons' Wars in the Reign of Edward II (1603)
The Owl (1604)
The Man in the Moon (1606)

The Legend of Thomas Cromwell, Earl of Essex (1607)
Poly-Olbion (1612 & 1622)
Idea (1619)
Pastorals: Containing Eclogues (1619)
Odes (1619)
The Battle of Agincourt (published 1627)
The Quest of Cynthia (published 1627)
Elegies Upon Sundry Occasions (1627)
Nymphidia, the Court of Fairy (1627)
The Shepherd's Sirena (1627)
Muses' Elysium (1630)
Moses' Birth and Miracles (1630)